Wise Church Planting wonderfully models dependent faith and Spirit-wrought vitality ...ry things its survey of churches, planted by real people in real contexts, shows us are needed. Dan Steel skilfully weaves together the experience of planters and a wealth of other resources to help everyone involved in church planting (especially the early stages) to lead scripturally, wisely and fruitfully. Dan's heart for people and for Jesus pastors you throughout. Recommended reading for planting teams and sending organisations alike.

Clive Bowsher
Director of Mission and Provost at Union School of Theology,
Bridgend, Wales

Ministry is hard. Church planting is uniquely hard. Too many church planting books lay out exciting, passionate plans to plant, but often lack a realism for those who put their hands to the plow. Dan Steel has done a wonderful service to the church planting world with this gem you hold in your hands. *Wise Church Planting* is that honest, real, and insightful book we have needed to fill the gap. The research and approach of this book is brilliant and highlights those able to teach us the most about church planting. That is, the practitioners who have done this work, experienced the difficulties, and own the scars of wisdom to help us. And do not think this book is limited to church planters. Every pastor should read this book if they too desire to avoid the pitfalls and landmines that come with all kinds of pastoral ministry.

Brian Croft
Executive Director, Practical Shepherding;
author, *Biblical Church Revitalization*

One of the most encouraging trends of the last twenty years has been the renewed commitment of evangelicals to church planting. However not every church plant that is attempted is successful. Drawing on his personal experience as a planter, and the results of an extensive survey of church planters, Dan Steel helpfully identifies some of the common reasons why church plants fail, and speaks the truths of Scripture into them. Above all else, he emphasises the need for church planters to exhibit Christian character and trust in God, rather than relying on their gifts, entrepreneurial skills and drive for success. The result is both challenging and hopeful. This book should be required reading for church planters and their teams, but would benefit everyone in church leadership because these dangers are not unique to church planting.

John Stevens
National Director, Fellowship of Independent
Evangelical Churches

Ministry is warfare. We go to battle against the desires of the flesh, the lies of the world, and the shortcoming's of God's people. Anyone who seeks to start a new church is stepping into that war but are they truly prepared for what is ahead of them? Dan Steel has put together an excellent field guide for church planters to help them recognize and avoid some of the most costly mistakes. Built on his research, experience, and study of scriptures, Dan doesn't simply identify the challenges but suggests ways to avoid them. I have no doubt that this book will prevent many men from falling into any one of these pitfalls so they might thrive in the trenches of a church planting ministry.

Matthew Spandler-Davison
Church in Hard Places Ministry Director

Dan addresses the most crucial component for pastors to consider when church planting, and that is wisdom! By focusing on both the internal character and external strategies necessary for healthy church plants, this is a book that should be required reading for all who are pursuing this noble call.

Ronnie Martin
Lead Pastor, Substance Church;
author, *Pastoring Small Towns*

WISE CHURCH PLANTING

Twelve Pitfalls to Avoid in Starting New Churches

DAN STEEL

FOREWORD BY J. A. MEDDERS

CHRISTIAN
FOCUS

10 9 8 7 6 5 4 3 2 1

Copyright © Dan Steel 2024
ISBN 978-1-5271-1101-1
ebook ISBN 978-1-5271-1145-5

Published in 2024
by
Christian Focus Publications Ltd,
Geanies House, Fearn, Ross-shire,
IV20 1TW, Great Britain.
www.christianfocus.com

Cover design: Daniel van Straaten

Printed and bound by
Bell and Bain, Glasgow

Contents

DEDICATION

*For Zoe, whose Christlike service
and loving partnership are a daily example to me.*

❧ ACKNOWLEDGMENTS ❧

One of my favourite blessings of the Kingdom of Jesus, is that we are not meant to live the Christian life alone. The same is true of this project and the book that has emerged from it – it really is the fruit of contributions from many folk around the world.

There are too many names to mention without it becoming something of a biblical genealogy, but I would be remiss to not say a particular thank you to encouragers and wise voices within multiple church planting networks, agencies, denominations and tribes. You've been willing to write a foreword (thanks Jeff!), help shape the questions, examine the results and consider the implications with me; to good friends and kind wordsmiths who have taken my clumsy sentences and messy grammar and made them something a little nicer to read; to dozens and dozens of planters from around the world who were willing to open up in vulnerability to a random pastor/planter/researcher from the UK and talk about their struggles; to leaders and church family at Magdalen Road Church, Oxford. Thank you for giving me the time and space to plod through, and for helping me process along the way; to new (very patient) friends at Christian Focus; to Ellie, Barney, Josh and Abi who, along with Zoe, have (fairly) happily let me go and hide in the 'shed' at the end of the garden and write.

❦ FOREWORD ❦

Church planters and church planting churches can glean theological and missiological lessons from the agricultural world.

In front of my house are three stare-worthy oak trees. They tower over the yard, providing plenty of shade for our grass and making a lovely community for a handful of birds. These growing oak trees are in an amoeba-shaped flower bed. We've had all kinds of flowers and plants in this bed—lilies, wax myrtles, society garlic—and nothing can survive. We put in new flowers and plants, and they don't make it after a few months. My wife and I dig, plant, fertilize, and spend money, but nothing works. The problem? The oaks. They are greedily taking all the water and not allowing enough sunlight for what is around them. No matter what we plant there, it won't make it. Church plants have these metaphorical-agricultural realities, too. Factors leading to failure.

Dan Steel has provided an agricultural-missiological autopsy on why church plants fail. You are holding a masterful and insightful work on the various conditions for why church plants don't make it. Dan's deep research—both with pastors and planters and the living Word of God—helps us learn the major factors for why church plants fail.

In his pastoral way, Dan explains the factors outside of a church plant—the 'oak trees'—that can hinder a church plant's longevity of faithful gospel ministry. And aside from external forces, there tend to be more problems within the plant. Internal battles, sins of the planter, and so forth. Dan has found multiple reasons on this front for why church plants struggle—and he has words of wisdom on these conditions.

The sovereignty of God keeps me sane. We rest in His power and grace in the work of church planting because, as the Chief Shepherd said, 'With man this is impossible, but with God all things are possible' (Matt. 19:26). A true disciple-making, Christ-exalting church is a work of the almighty God. And the Almighty chooses to use us. Paul reminds us that we can either be useful or unusable servants in the ministry. He tells us that we can make ourselves useful to the Lord in the work of ministry by purifying ourselves and becoming ready for good works (2 Tim. 2:21). Dan's work shows us how internal and external hindrances hurt our usefulness, faithfulness, and fruitfulness in church planting.

My recommendation as you read: Read wisely. Slowly. Every church planter should seriously consider what is in these pages. Every church planting church should evaluate their greenhouse and see how they can set up their planters to flourish. Lastly, be ready to pick up a shovel, dig a drain, fertilize, remove thorns and invasive and aggressive hindrances, repent, raise money, relocate, dial back, and do whatever you need to do. Plant a church that's useful to the Master. Be a planter who is ready to be used by Jesus. Our Father is a master gardener. He will prune so that you can bear much fruit. May this book be a tool in the risen Christ's hands to help your plant flourish for decades.

J.A. Medders, Houston, Texas
September, 2023

🌿 INTRODUCTION 🌿

I love the local church. Counter-cultural communities born of, shaped by, and built around, the gospel of Christ. Points of light, hope, and love in a dark, divided, and increasingly cynical world. We need churches. We need more churches.

For the last twenty-five years, church plants have largely shaped my experience of church: first as part of a core team launching with the mess of seventeen people squashed into a front room, fold-out chairs, green carpet, printed orders of service; then seven years later as a planter in the same city, as the front room became a school dining hall, which then became a sports hall. When no one else could be squashed into that space we planted again, thirty-six adults and five kids meeting in a different part of town. Years later, as the senior pastor of another church, we've seen the need of neighbourhoods where there's little gospel witness and responded by sending our own people. Our church has planted two other churches directly, and has also been involved in a number of other collaborative projects. Church planting has shaped my experience of church and, in many ways, it has shaped me too.

We need churches. We need more churches. In this book, I am trying to pick apart how and why it is that plants go wrong (or, at least, don't go as right as we'd hoped). Let me state two things at the outset: (1) I'm certainly not writing as an expert, but rather one who's had the privilege of speaking to lots of planters and (2) please don't read it as a book that 'points fingers'. It's not meant to be read with your inner voice of disappointment and frustration, but rather as a friend from within the planting world, wanting to help strengthen our efforts, wanting to raise some questions that might help avoid some of the pain along the way.

Chilli plants

Our house is tall, narrow, and on the outskirts of Oxford, with three floors but built onto a slight hill and so it ends up as six levels. The top level (where our youngest sleeps) is an early-afternoon suntrap, and for this reason it often doubles as a make-shift greenhouse with windowsills bustling with plants. At the moment we're propagating a selection of chilli seedlings but even though they all came from the same seed packets—and were planted at the same time—it's obvious which are thriving, growing, and flourishing. I'm not sure why. Perhaps the seeds themselves were from different parent plants? Perhaps greenfly and other pests have had a part to play? Perhaps the micro-climate on the windowsills or even the competition for sunlight between some of the plants has been a factor, but it's clear that some are not going to produce chillis and will end up on the compost heap at the end of the garden.

This book is an effort to work out some of the reasons why church plants–that may on paper look hopeful—don't thrive. It's based upon an attempt to gather stories from struggling planters from around the world (both those whose plants have closed but also those who are 'limping along') and then to analyse common threads of why that has happened.

Numbers and research

The number of struggling church plants (and planters) out there may surprise you. One often-quoted piece of research by the North American Mission Board found that after one year 99 per cent of plants were still active, by two years 92 per cent, by the third year 81 per cent, but by the fourth year only 68 per cent. Almost a third failed to make it[1]. To be honest, those numbers sound high from our context in Western Europe. Many plants will struggle and limp along. But that kind of huge drop-off rate isn't something I've seen here or found in the research project that sits behind this study.

The problem with evangelism?

A critique that is often levelled at the church more generally is that it is only really interested in making new converts. The easy task (in one sense) is to prayerfully, expectantly, share the message of Christ and see fruit by way of new converts. The trouble is, however, that the risen, ascended, and authoritative Lord Jesus didn't call us to only make converts, but rather to …

> … make disciples of all nations, baptizing them in the name of the Father and of the Son and of the Holy Spirit, and teaching them to obey everything I have commanded you. And surely I am with you always, to the very end of the age (Matt. 28:19-20).

To simply get people 'into the kingdom' and not help them to mature and grow and flourish, is to start the task of discipleship and then walk off, leaving these 'baby' Christians to fend for themselves unattended. It was never meant to be this way. As any parent will tell you, the job of raising and maturing a child is a huge privilege, an awesome responsibility, and a lot of hard work.

---

1. Quoted in Ed Stetzer and Warren Bird, Viral Churches (Jossey-Bass, 2014) p. 104

I wonder if our inability to properly disciple people has a parallel in church planting? We expend vast amounts of energy in launching and getting the thing going: dreaming, vision-setting, recruiting, fundraising, making websites, printing and marketing, and then don't give the support and care needed to help the church – the disciples – actually thrive. Remember the study? Nearly one third don't last four years.

Many have commented on the difficulties of church leadership in the West, and the ease with which we can be shaped in our ministries and expectations by the way everyone else around us does things. Like the battle with the supermarket shopping trolley that keeps veering to one side, it's a constant challenge to minister in a way that reflects the life and values of Jesus when the values around us are pulling us in the opposite direction. Too easily we can value what the world values. Zack Eswine's *Imperfect Pastor* has been particularly helpful for me in battling the drift in ministry mindset.

> As you enter ministry, you will be tempted to orient your desires toward doing large things in famous ways as fast and as efficiently as you can. But take note. A crossroads waits for you. Jesus is that crossroads. Because almost anything in life that truly matters will require you to do small, mostly overlooked things, over a long period of time with Him. The pastoral vocation, because it focuses on helping people cultivate what truly matters, is therefore no exception.[2]

The problem is that church planting, in the words of Eswine, is very often about 'large, famous and fast.' When the clock is ticking, and funding is only for a limited season, the pressure for 'success' can be debilitating. It is often felt

---

2. Zack Eswine, *The Imperfect Pastor: Discovering Joy in Our Limitations through a Daily Apprenticeship with Jesus* (Crossway, 2015) p. 26.

that the pastor needs to grow the church, to raise the funds needed to be self-sufficient.

Market Research

When I was a part of the core team of the church that started in a front room with green carpet, I worked for a nearby market research company that helped global clients understand how they were perceived, and why, by the general public. In our introductory training we were warned in the first couple of weeks that we would never be able to watch TV adverts in the same way again. They were right. My family will tell you how annoying it is. My company showed us how adverts work—the combination of story, emotional engagement and branding—and so now whenever I see, hear, or read any kind of advertising, I'm analysing it. It's annoying for me too.

But it also means I like asking questions and trying to dig into the reasons why people do what they do or think what they think, or how they feel about something. Trying to see the big picture and make a narrative out of the numbers. Which is where this project came from. It was an itch starting in the spring of 2018 that never went away: was there a way that I could talk to a broad selection of planters about how they have struggled and find out why?

That started a series of conversations, which led to an online survey, some follow-up conversations, and resulted in eighty stories from planters and pastors all over the world (the questions I asked are in Appendix 1). With eighty stories, it sits somewhere in between a quantitative (numbers-based) and qualitative (descriptive-based) study – not really enough data for me to make confident statistical analyses, but more in-depth accounts than we would usually get for a qualitative study. I have sought to bolster and supplement the stories I collected with other material that is available – from a handful of books covering similar topics (published and unpublished), some reports that have been commissioned, as well as a few Ph.D. studies with a level of overlap.

A tangled ball of wool

In exploring and analysing the stories, it's clear that each church plant is a unique combination of factors: the local context, the personalities, gifting and character of the people involved, as well as their prior ministry experiences and expectations. While there are common themes and threads that seem to unite many of these stories and interviews, there is still complexity. The analogy I've found most helpful is that each struggling plant is like a tangled ball of wool made up of multiple colours. As you seek to carefully unpick the ball in question, you'll find that each one is unique, comprised of different colours and threads. On average each plant listed 4.3 factors that were causing them to struggle (though one listed nine!). This project is an attempt to carefully pull apart and examine twelve of the main factors of why plants don't thrive: twelve common pitfalls.

Each chapter examines each strand within five sections:

1. A hypothetical story element helps us see how easy it might be to fall into this pitfall. These aren't 'real' but rather draw from a variety of accounts and examples.
2. An exploration of the study itself. What did this issue actually look like in the words of the planters? I'll be deliberately quoting verbatim from the study within this section, seeking to give a voice to many whose stories haven't been heard.
3. What Scriptures can help us as we think about each issue? What truths do we need to engage with and consider from the Bible?
4. An opportunity for self-examination. Are there helpful questions we need to personally engage with

around this strand? Whether you're a planter, or part of a core team, or a pastor sending out a plant, what questions should you be asking? The questions could be both focussed for the individual but also usefully asked of the whole group.

5. How have others dealt well with this issue? What strategies might we consider as we seek both to make ourselves aware of potential issues and to handle them faithfully? Here we will hear from pastors around the globe who have wrestled with this issue and hear how they dealt with it.

There's also a final section that will help us think about where we might go from here, as well as how we can care for people when it all goes wrong. A few individuals I spoke to had been caught up in the mess of a church plant that had to close, and it was clearly still very painful. Indeed 44 per cent of people said they felt they hadn't received enough support during the difficult months of the plant, or after it had closed.

Let me reiterate: please read this book as coming from a friend from within the planting world, wanting to help strengthen our efforts, and avoid some of the needless pain of planting churches. Also, please read with hope. Not hope because 'if we just'— if we just adjust this aspect of planting, or train better in that, or recruit the perfect core team, then it will all be good—but hope because of the gospel. Hope because our God has promised to build His church, and because He has prepared in advance for us good works to walk in (Eph. 2:10). A hope, not because of us, but because our God is faithful.

Six Internal Pitfalls: Inside the Planter and the Church

PITFALL 1

❦ CHARACTER ❦

ADMIRING GIFTING OVER GODLINESS DERAILS PLANTERS AND PLANTS

THE STORY

Since university days when he had been encouraged into giving a couple of evangelistic talks, it had been strongly suggested to Greg that he ought to consider some kind of paid Christian ministry. It was only in recent years that church planting had come onto his radar, indeed this seemed to be what almost all of his contemporaries were hoping to do. People appreciated what he had to say and how he said it and so an increasing number of opportunities for 'up-front' ministry kept coming his way. He had always had what his mum called, 'the gift of the gab,' and behind the pulpit he felt in his element; he felt this was what he ought to do with his life. Behind closed doors, however, he knew that there were complications. That was where his niggling doubts were loudest.

As his sending church began to train him, and he trawled through various questionnaires and assessment forms with different church planting networks, he became increasingly adept at being *suitably elusive* when difficult or awkward questions came his way. He assumed everyone struggled with anger like he did and, anyway, if God was blessing his ministry (and clearly He was) then issues of character couldn't be that important? Could they?

The plant began and, as is often the case, things were busy and bountiful in the first few months. Lots of events and outreach opportunities, lots of other local Christians heard about it and a number jumped over to join the project. People particularly loved Greg and his preaching style. As things were growing, Greg was thriving, but leadership meetings were becoming more fraught. It all really started when one of the other leaders, alongside lots of warmth and positivity, had sensitively offered a couple of thoughts about how services and sermons might be improved. The emotions in the room charged very quickly and comments went down like a lead balloon. Greg quickly responded in anger, clearly defensive and annoyed. They decided it would be best to park it until next time, but future meetings resulted in short fuses and tempers and walking on egg-shells. Greg slowly distanced himself from any who might want to 'push-back' on his ideas or ministry. Privately, relationships began to unravel and within twelve months things came to a head. Greg started something new on the other side of town, and half the church, those who had been his biggest fans and closest friends, went too. Last thing the leadership heard was that, sadly, something similar happened a few years later.

The Study

The nature of Church ministry on its own can be both an illuminating and a refining process, even more so the adventure of church planting. As we're pushed out of our comfort zones and recognise more of the mess within us, and that our motives are always mixed, we are pushed to depend upon God rather than ourselves. In his book, Tom

Bennardo outlines a number of truths related to church planting, problems with the process or culture of planting and yet he begins in chapter 1, with the truth that the foundational problem of planting 'lies with you' ... he speaks of the reality of arrogance that he's seen in many planters:

> Call your motivation to plant a church whatever you like – entrepreneurship, a pioneering spirit, holy discontent. But somewhere in the mix lies the presumption that you possess a superior way, superior skills, superior drive, or all three. You wouldn't become a church planter if it weren't so.[1]

The issue of individual character problems and faults came up in 44 per cent of the stories we heard. It was one of the main reasons for church plants faltering. Respondents were extraordinarily honest and vulnerable as they shared some of the painful truths about themselves that the planting process had brought to the fore. The topic was expressed in a variety of different ways:

1. A number mentioned that through the pain, they had come to realise (or remember again) that before they are a church planter or gospel minister, they are first and foremost a child of God; that knowing God is not just an idea or a theory but daily enjoying real relationship with Him is vital; that knowing Him, not just knowing about Him, is crucial to life first, and then ministry. For many, the process of planting had revealed deficiencies in their grasp of their fundamental identity. It had also shown them that the need to feed themselves first, before seeking to feed others, is foundational.

---

1. Tom Bennardo, *The Honest Guide to Church Planting* (Z Carr, 2019), p23

What was the main thing you learned? ...

- To take care of others, you have to take care of yourself.

- Being a disciple of Jesus is first and foremost. You can't expect to recreate what you're not living.

- How much I can endure, and that I have to be diligent with the discipline of feeding myself first.

2. A number reflected that they had discovered more about themselves and the depths of their own sin and fallibility, as well as deficiencies in their gifting (we'll explore this more exhaustively in Chapter 4), and the impact that this self-discovery had upon others within the plant.

- I realised I'm an optimistic, headstrong, impatient, talkative, ideas guy.

- If I did it again, I would work out my junk before I planted [...] I'm a Gordon Ramsay personality type. Angry every six months and it boils over.

- I was overly determined, worked too much, came across harsh to people ... If I disagreed with my co-worker on an issue, I would typically just do it my way.

- I was confronted with my own weakness and inability.

- I had too much confidence in my own ability.

- The main cause of my demise? Accusers called me a bully and narcissist.

- There were unfortunately moral issues with the person I looked to as my co-planter. I had my suspicions, I had the notion that our relationship was not transparent, but I did not have any evidence of wrongdoing. Once I had that evidence it became obvious that we could not continue, at least not without repentance and evidence of repentance.

3. Others, however, could now more clearly see their own weakness and insufficiencies, but in so doing had beautifully learnt about the strength and sufficiency of Christ for them. Even though planting had been (or still was) a hard and painful experience, it had gloriously led them to trust in Christ more deeply, rather than in self. Whilst they thought they were forming a new church plant, actually Christ was forming them.

What did I learn?

- I struggle with fear and anxiety. This has been the greatest blessing of church planting. Since coming to more clearly understand this about myself, I have come to better understand how God's grace through Christ is sufficient for my profound weakness. I have a lot more 'stick-to-it-ness' than I thought.

- My identity comes from Christ. I knew that, but I think I get it more.

- How far I can be stretched. I learned a lot about stress and emotional health. I learned about dependence on God and His power.

- My sin is complex and great. Jesus is simple and greater.

- I'm weak but God can empower me.

Again, this idea is picked up by Bennardo, who, expanding on Paul's *'Thorn in the Flesh'* autobiography in 2 Corinthians 12, coins the helpful phrase, 'the process of perpetual weakening'[2]. He explains that in his experience, it's not simply that God *weakens* us for a season before revealing that He can deal with it and make us strong again, but rather that our kind Father in Heaven, in His love for us and to keep us from trusting in self, deliberately, continually and perpetually weakens His children, that we might not depend upon ourselves, but have to run to Him for daily strengthening. God loves us too much to think that we're enough.

4. It's clear that some planters were still reflecting and dealing with the personal damage that planting had caused, or still was causing them. When asked how it had affected them, they answered:

- So far – how vulnerable I am.

- Still figuring that out, but I'm really hurting.

Others have seen the importance of the need for personal holiness.

- There will be times when you can make excuses for lacking in resources, people and finance, but there is never an excuse for lacking in prayer, faith, and holiness.

THE SCRIPTURES
Scripturally speaking, the role of the church planter (although admittedly never named!) is perhaps synonymous with the role of a pioneer evangelist: an individual (or team) taking

---

2. Bennardo, p. 30.

the message of Christ into new territory and seeking for that gospel to bear fruit in individuals, who in turn form a local body—a church with leadership. While this *is* still evident in our times – and a number of pioneer evangelists supported by various mission agencies and planting networks took part in the study – much modern-day planting looks a little less pioneering and a little more like starting ready-made smaller churches in new areas where there is no (or little) witness.

The role of church leader (or pastor and elder) in the Bible is clearly established within a number of poignant passages that ought to be carefully studied by any church planting team. A church planter is certainly not *less* than a pastor or an elder, though, with the added pressure and responsibilities that planting brings, he may need to be more.

1 Timothy 3:1-7 and Titus 1:5-9 are important texts to grapple with.

Notice a number of aspects:

First of all, an elder is to be exemplary in managing himself and his family. As Paul writes, the weight of these descriptions has much more to do with who a person is before the Lord – faithfulness in daily living – rather than in what they can do in a church.

The Puritan pastor and author, Richard Baxter, talks of the pastor having oversight over himself and the importance of managing his own family, before he can manage God's family (1 Tim. 3:5). For example, he is to be blameless—above reproach, faithful to his spouse and have children that are faithful or obedient. This doesn't call for perfection, but it does perhaps call for progress. His is not to be a divided, chaotic household, but rather one in which there is peace and obedience. He is to stand apart from the surrounding culture and so, in a place like Crete which was renowned for bad behaviour, not be overbearing, or quick-tempered, or given to drunkenness, or violent, or pursuing dishonest gain, but rather one who loves what is good, who is self-controlled, upright, holy and disciplined.

It's striking that where *we* often look for competency or gifting—Is this person entrepreneurial? Can this person hold a room? Do people follow him?—Paul is seemingly much more interested in character and godliness.

Secondly, you must also have a good reputation with those outside the church (1 Tim. 3:7), as well as having the gift of hospitality (1 Tim. 3:2 and Titus 1:8). Often Christian leaders can slip into the problem of only spending time with other believers, however, these verses imply good relationships with those outside the church family. Perhaps this is especially true in church planting? For example, when we imagine the gift of hospitality in the twenty-first century it can be easy to think of a dinner party, a candlelit meal with good conversation, excellent food, and napkins. In the Bible (as indeed with much of the Middle East today), hospitality has much more to do with kindness and a costly welcome shown to a stranger. In often dangerous territory it's extravagant love and protection for the outsider and the refugee, with no expectation of reciprocation. It's the kind of underserved love that God shows to us. In planting it may well be that this aspect of welcome and hospitality is especially important in the life of a young church. If the planter is cold or relationally distant that can be a significant barrier to the church functioning well.

Thirdly, it's not just about character: there must be an ability to teach. Because Jesus governs His church by His word, the pastor must be able to feed the flock by opening up the living Word. Hence, in Timothy he is to be able to teach (1 Tim. 3:2), and in Titus he must hold firmly to the trustworthy message as it has been taught, so that he can encourage others by sound doctrine and refute those who oppose it (Titus 1:9).

There are other passages that bring out aspects of what it means to be a pastor including from Acts 20, 1 Timothy 5 and 1 Peter 5. We'll look at these, alongside Titus 1 and 1 Timothy 3, more carefully in the self-examination section below.

SELF EXAMINATION

These questions can be used for personal reflection, but also can productively be used within a smaller group. Where you see the word 'you' that can work as both a singular and a plural!

1. Read through Titus 1, 1 Timothy 2 and 1 Peter 5. Where do you have most doubts that you are qualified to serve as a planter/pastor/elder? Discuss and pray through these with another leader or mentor.

2. Be honest, what mixed motives do you have for planting a church?

3. How much have you prayed regarding the shaping of your church plant?

4. How will you feel if your church plant does not thrive?

SUCCESSES AND STRATEGIES

... in Christ we speak before God with sincerity ... (2 Cor. 2:17).

These words from Paul get to the heart of authentic ministry: in Christ, before God, with sincerity. But these words also get to the heart of the character issues that have beset my ministry. Particularly in the early days of planting I was living the opposite. It would have been accurate to write, 'In church I spoke before people with hypocrisy.'

There was no flagrant sin, no private addiction, no public shame. But there wasn't much sincerity. Outwardly I was doing all the right things: leading planting meetings, teaching and preaching God's Word, building relationships and trust within the community. If you'd met me I probably would have been able to convince you that it was all 'authentic.' But inwardly it was all out of whack. I was finding my identity in being 'a church planter' rather than being 'in Christ.' I was fearing the opinions of the people who'd sacrificed lots to join us, or given lots to support us, instead of embracing a posture of fearing the Lord. And so I was ministering out of a hypocrisy that was inviting people into something that I myself wasn't living out.

Here's what I found: You can live that way for a while and just about scrape by. But when things get hard in ministry, that kind of hypocrisy is a cistern that's cracked and dry. When people get hard to love, and the community gets hard to reach, and the cost gets significant for you personally, without sincerity there's little chance of longevity.

And here's what the Lord graciously taught me: 'fear of man will prove to be a snare ...' (Prov. 29:25). A snare that not only hampers me, but through me hamstrings our whole church plant. But 'the fear of the LORD is a fountain of life ...' (Prov. 14:27). A fount not only for me, but through me flowing to our whole church plant.

In Christ, before God, with sincerity, has become a fountain of life. What other people see on the outside may not have changed much at all. But before God and what He sees, and within me and how it feels, everything's changed. There's a joy in just being in Christ. There's a freedom in just speaking before God. And there's a safety just living in sincerity.

Andy Prime
Gracemount Community Church,
Edinburgh, UK

Further reading for this chapter
- Thabiti Anyabwile, *Finding Faithful Elders and Deacons*, (Crossway, 2012).
- Ray Ortlund and Sam Allberry, *You're not Crazy* (Crossway, 2023).

PITFALL 2

🔥 CHARACTER: PEOPLE AND PLACE 🔥

Sometimes character issues emerge later in the work often through interpersonal issues and burnout

THE STORY

To be encouraged to consider planting in his mid-twenties had been both an extraordinary challenge and an immense privilege for Joel. He still remembers the unexpected conversation with his senior pastor and still almost blushes to think about it. Having been involved at the heart of church life, he had proven himself to be a faithful and diligent worker over a number of years since graduating from university. He was always the first one in and the last one out, always with a to-do list that felt unhealthily long, and, if you looked carefully, always seemed to have that slightly run-down look. But that was ministry, wasn't it? He remembers a previous pastor saying he didn't want to waste his life—he would rather burn out, than rust out. Churches don't run themselves, do they?!

The months leading up to the plant had been busy and fraught, with a few key people pulling out before things had even got to launch stage. Joel had ended up being the key recruiter, fundraiser, venue hirer, project manager, leaflet delivery guy, and general visionary/dogsbody. As the 'behind-closed-doors' soft-launch happened, then the public family fun-day followed by an Easter invitation service, he would joke that adrenaline, caffeine, and the Holy Spirit were his secrets! Though, if he was being really honest, he suspected the first two might be more important.

Fast-forward twelve months in and he was tired. Really tired. Perhaps more tired than he had ever been, but, despite strong suggestions from other concerned pastors, he struggled to let anyone else get too involved. It was his job, wasn't it? And anyway, he wasn't sure they would want to be involved, and anyway, how could you know if they would do the job well? It was just easier for him to get it done and get it done right. But it turned out that as the church and the complexity of the project grew, so there just weren't enough hours in the day. Burning the candle at both ends only gets you so far, and the more you burn the less sleep you end up with, and the less sleep you end up with the more exhausted you get. And suddenly you're twenty months in and you're not really yourself anymore, and your joy has gone, and you're getting some strange physical symptoms, and so, after a number of medical tests, your doctor recommends taking an extended time away.

THE STUDY

Like many relationships, we are usually on our best behaviour in the early days, seeking to make a good impression. It's only a few months (or years!) down the line that some of our bad habits and quirks come out, as the mask slips and the truth is out of the bag. That reality may be a slightly quicker experience in the life of a church planter. The pressure cooker of planting—with its associated anxiety and stress—and the sheer weight of the project make ideal conditions for mask-slippage.

Of the planters we spoke to whose churches had actually closed, 54 per cent lasted for more than five years, showing that plants don't usually shut quickly (21 per cent in under three years). Perhaps it takes time for the deficiencies of the planter (or the processes) to develop in unhealthy ways. Fruit, however unhealthy, takes time to grow.

A number spoke honestly of the tendency towards burnout that resulted from a variety of factors, here they are boiled down into two pieces of advice:

1. You need to find your people

Planting is busy work and, day to day, planters are easily isolated. They need support from others, both inside and outside the church they've planted. Too many spoke of their lack of friendships, and of loneliness:

- I need the ideas and help of others more than I appreciated when I was an Associate Pastor on staff at a mega-church where those people were also on staff. I need to be a part of a team of dedicated men who are planting together.

- I need to partner with others who are church planters, not just those from my church, but others to help me grow and to also help with training resources.

- Planting a church is hard work which requires a team spirit.

- Do your homework beforehand if you are looking to plant in an area. Plant with networks that you can theologically align with. Have support systems around you because planting is a lonely and difficult ministry.'

- I need other people to thrive—planting is lonely.

- Be healthy: emotionally, spiritually, relationally (especially with your spouse), and morally. The pressure is so great that it will tear your world apart. Make sure you have healthy boundaries and accountability.

From my experience of planting in Birmingham, UK, we unwittingly stumbled across a winning combination with two of us set aside as pastors. At the beginning as we launched, I was the more full-time of the two of us, while my colleague was finishing theological training. There are several reasons why it worked so well between us: we shared a strong underlying friendship; we were united in core theological convictions; and we were (and are) quite different in terms of temperament, personality, and gifting. In the short term, diversity within unity is not uncomplicated, but in the long term it is good news. A few years in, as it became clear that my own household might need to move elsewhere to be nearer wider family, I stepped back in terms of hours, and he stepped up to be more full-time. Now, in Birmingham there is a cohort system (https://2020birmingham.org.uk) whereby planters from across the denominational spectrum gather weekly to support and encourage one another in wider plans and to collaborate with plant churches all over the city. Isolation and loneliness are exhausting, and these two things lead to pastors burning out. You need to find your people – friendships – from both inside your plant, but also outside.

2. You need to find your pace

Alongside the isolation, a number spoke of an all-consuming 'workaholism' or a 'perfectionism.' They reported that this was seen in a failure to plan well for the longer-term. It was also seen in an inability either to say 'no' when asked to be involved in something, or to actively delegate and release others into ministry. Finally, it manifested itself in a constant and powerful feeling of frustration with others who are part of the project but don't seem to care as much. If church planting is a race at the athletic track, it was as if at launch day the gun went and they began sprinting: arms and legs pumping, stride lengthening, but then failed to realise it wasn't 100m. Turns out church planting is more like running an ultra-marathon (with numerous obstacles) than a sprint.

- Learn to say 'no' from the beginning. Protect the vision and direction of the church while you inculcate a healthy DNA. Then give stuff away to like-minded leaders who emerge.

- Don't do everything. Do a few things well. Specialize before you diversify.

- Drink lots of water. Get eight hours of sleep every night. Exercise. Read. Pray.

- I get frustrated at people easily. I get frustrated when others don't have the same passion to see something happen as I do, and that is not good. I have a hard time dealing with people who are apathetic, who know to do good ... and don't. I need a distance from some of the 'work' of ministry to simply be free to love and minister to those under my charge. I don't do well with people who have ideas/opinions who are not going to step out and do the work to see those ideas come to reality.'

This latter one is common, and not just among planters but in any ministry. As we explored in Chapter 1, it is easy to find our identity in wrong things. This is a daily battle, as our hearts constantly veer towards self and away from Christ, towards finding a sense of worth in what 'I' have done rather than what Christ has done. It's often almost imperceptible, but it can be very damaging both for the planter and the plant.

One conversation with a planter in Australia who, among other things, burnt out from over-activity, was especially helpful. Having reached the point where he needed to take time away, when he thought and sought the Lord as to why he was so exhausted he realised (much to his surprise) that he was now barely, in practice, preaching the gospel of grace. Instead, it was all about activity. Of course, he would tick the doctrine box saying that he believed in grace, was justified by grace, saved by grace, loved grace, and that he knew that grace changes everything … On paper he was in the right place, but then (following a number of frustrations within the plant) he could see within himself and his preaching an unhealthy anger and activism. Upon reflection, he realised that this had come to shape not only his ministry and preaching, but also the wider culture of the church.

Grace is more than a box we tick or an idea that we subscribe to: it's a truth we must build our lives and our ministries upon daily. Our church plants are not about us. Grace brings humility, which leads to the revelation that we're not perfect, and that we need others to support us. It also means learning how to release others to serve, how to pace ourselves, and indeed, how to rest.

THE SCRIPTURES
A shadow-side to the 'ideal' church planter?
The slow and steady attrition of ministry life is painful. As we've seen, within the study there were not that many

early 'blow-ups' (within the first couple of years) where a planter had to pull out or a plant pulled the plug, but instead a number of slower collapses a few years in. An element that exacerbates this is that many networks and denominations have a particular view of what a church planter ought to look like: entrepreneurial, strong, rugged, visionary, individualistic. Think bloody-minded resilience. Think (often bearded?) pioneer. Taken in isolation, these are good qualities, the problem, though, is that such personalities often have a 'shadow-side': a pridefulness and independence, the fruit of which, some years down the line, will often be messy.

The fruit of pride

One of the constant drumbeats of the Bible is that God opposes the proud but gives grace to the humble (for example Prov. 3:34, James 4:6, 1 Pet. 5:5), and when God repeats something, it's worth listening to. It's a reality modelled especially in the life of Jesus, who 'throughout all his life' laid down what was rightfully His as He sought to serve His people. This life of service and self-denial finds its nadir and acme in His death on the cross, a cursed death, which He underwent on their behalf, before being raised again to give them new life (Phil. 2:5-11). He is the model counter-cultural leader par excellence who came 'not to be served, but to serve, and to give up his life as a ransom for many' (Mark 10:45). The line between entrepreneurial, visionary church planting and arrogance may be a fine one at times, but it's vital that we spot it.

One of the core tenets for any pastor or planter must be a humble acknowledgement of the fact that God's power is made perfect through our weakness (2 Cor. 12:9). Yet, in leadership, (especially when a church is just starting out and people can be anxious about whether the fragile young 'seedling' will even make it) it can be very difficult to actually admit weakness and vulnerability. In some cultures more than others this is especially the case. Church planters would do well to regularly ask careful questions as to where their model for leadership actually comes from, and whether it has more in common with overbearing, lording-it-over, CEO-business leaders or military managers, than with a humble king who, for the joy set before Him, died the death of a criminal. We're called to follow Him, to daily die to self.

The fruit of isolation

Another unhelpful 'shadow-side' of the rugged individualism can easily be a functional isolationism that can result in (at least) two further dangers:

- Planting (as with any type of leadership) can by nature be a lonely existence. Quite apart from the extreme busyness and activity—which can leave little time for friendships (whether inside or outside the church body) —there are few who really understand the manifold pressures and anxieties that planting can bring. Ideally though, ministry is a communal activity, whether it be that the New Testament model for eldership is a plurality (for example Acts 14:23; 16:4; 20:17 or 21:18), or simply the diverse model that Paul sets us as he often greets and commends a breadth of individuals and teams with whom he's ministered (see for example Rom. 16:1-16).

- Another (almost paradoxical) fruit of individualism can be a lack of desire (or ability) to pour into, train and release others. Again, the example of Paul is one to consider, as we watch him deliberately investing in and releasing younger ministers into ministry. Whether it be his example in encouraging both Timothy and Titus to invest in others (see for example 2 Tim. 2:2 or Titus 2:1-8), God calls His people not to be dams that store up, but rather streams that abundantly bless others. We're not to be those who cling onto the things that God gives us; instead, we are to pass His gifts on in open-handed generosity to others. Often the problem for the individualist is that they struggle with an overly-controlling model of leadership and are unwilling to release and let others go.

SELF-EXAMINATION

These questions can be used for personal reflection, but also can productively be used within a smaller group. Where you see the word 'you', that can work as both a singular and a plural!

1. What has God been teaching you since you launched …? about (1) yourself, (2) Himself, (3) church ministry and (4) church planting?

2. If you've not yet launched, what has He been teaching you in the last six months?

3. Do you have friends with whom you can relax? Do you have someone in place (whether from inside the plant or outside) who is able to ask you hard questions about how you're really doing? Who? When did they last do this?!

4. What problems and challenges have you faced since you launched? How could you have dealt with them better?

SUCCESSES AND STRATEGIES

The longer-term fallout from ongoing internal character issues will lead to a mix of external symptoms – some of which will be explored in future chapters.

Our church plant took ten years to get off the ground. We encountered two problems that kept sinking the church plant like a balloon being pulled further and further underwater by a weight.

First, the church plant was delayed due to a teammate's character failure. His character had not been proven long enough before being sent to the mission field. He disqualified himself within the first nine months on the field. The sin brought shame to the name of Jesus and slowed down the advance of the gospel. By the grace of God, he was convicted by the Spirit and repented of his sin. But we found ourselves church planting alone.

The second delay was due to interpersonal conflict that lasted seven long years. The issues were varied. Often it was just plain not thinking the best about someone else. Our family acted more like the culture in which we lived, while our teammates did not. This rubbed them the wrong way. The people in our cultural context compared us and highlighted our linguistic abilities and cultural acquisition. This was grating upon our co-workers. I was more proactive in approaching friends to read the Bible while my teammate didn't feel he had the chance to ask because I already had. They felt I was excluding them from Bible studies.

The issues piled on, but we were often unaware. After a season, it would blow up. We attempted to solve the conflict, but the pattern was not broken. What we don't repair we repeat, and it happened over and over again. The gospel advance slowed. There was no unity. We were divided and seemingly fighting against each other. Envy and rivalry had prevailed. Someone outside looking in could likely say there was no love among us.

The conflict came to a head, and our co-workers made the decision to depart from our ministry context without resolving the disunity. We were discouraged and beat up. I wanted to quit church planting. However, within a few months of our teammates' departure, we began to see spiritual fruit. Friends turned to Christ, were baptized, and added to the church. Our church covenanted together and there was real unity. The gospel was advancing in our city. Unity, it seems, is just as miraculous as the signs and wonders performed by the Apostles in Acts. Without unity, the gospel advance slows.

Pastor T
Northern Spain

Further reading for this chapter

- Paul Tripp, *Lead* (Crossway, 2020)
- Jeramie Rinne, *Church Elders: How to Shepherd God's People Like Jesus* (Crossway, 2014)

PITFALL 3

✹ DISUNITY ✹

A staggering number of planters identify disunity as a major pitfall

THE STORY

From day one, John was thrilled at the beautiful diversity of the core plant team.

The town they were prayerfully planning to plant into was the next one over from their sending church, with not much by way of gospel witness for a city of that size. With a university right at the centre, as well as areas of deprivation and new flats for those in the business community, their prayerful longing had always been to gather an initial group that would, as best they could, reflect the diverse reality of the area. Which, ideally, meant an early mix in economic, educational and ethnic terms. Add to that a number of people already living in the area, who, when they heard on the grapevine about the plans quickly jumped on board (some quickly jumping ship from their churches) and there was a healthy-sized base to start from. It was a stunning opportunity to show a cynical watching world something of the uniting power of the gospel, to show that Jesus is for all kinds of people; a modern-day Ephesian church with 'dividing walls of hostility' removed. At least, that was the hope.

Fairly soon into the project though, the daily challenges of a diverse community began to take over. There were some theological questions, but the disagreements were mainly cultural. It turns out everyone seemed to have an opinion on everything; service style (some wanted more liturgy, organisation and structure, others didn't want to be 'bound by tradition'), music (too loud, too quiet, too traditional, too contemporary, drums), food (some were gluten free, vegan, and concerned to minimise carbon footprints, while others just really wanted as much and as often as possible), or dress-code (smart or casual or somewhere in between?) to preaching style (questions over length of sermon, vocabulary used, appropriateness of sports illustrations). All too quickly the dream of a beautifully diverse-but-unified body ended up being more of a nightmare with different factions all eventually turning on the planter. Things did not end well.

In the years to come when the dust had settled, the planter's 'autopsy' of the project picked up on both his initial naivety (we all love the idea of an eclectic gospel community until real people turn up with ideas and beliefs that are different from ours), but also a neglect in teaching the church how to practically (non-judgmentally) understand one another and live in a loving community. What does it actually mean to put others' needs before our own? How do we use and relinquish our gospel freedoms for the sake of others? What does it mean to be those who serve rather than seeking to always be served? In a world where we're polite but, very often, people only really associate with others like them (or indeed others they like), learning how to bear with brothers and sisters who are not like you, is hard.

THE STUDY

From the study, sadly, but perhaps unsurprisingly, all kinds of disunity problems were evident; indeed 63 per cent of the stories I heard mentioned one form (or more) of disunity that was described as being significantly detrimental to the health of the plant. Of that 63 per cent there were divisions over four main aspects:

- 13 per cent encountered disunity over the **ministry philosophy** of the plant

- 18 per cent spoke of a disunity regarding **authority** (questions over who's in charge)

- 36 per cent disunity regarding **theological** issues

- 42 per cent mentioned a **relational** disunity

In their own words …

Ministry Philosophy

- It seems that some of the original core group were not that excited about planting a church in a new area, but wanted a church to escape to. This meant they didn't quite grasp the vision. It also meant that they disengaged from church life/mission somewhat, bringing tension and discouragement to others.

- … differences in understanding of what an essential working class church meeting should look like.

- In a way that I know falls somewhat short of the depth of it all, I know that the disunity derived from issues of small-town church, big city megachurch ministry philosophies.

Authority

- There were some members who had challenges in submitting to my leadership.

- There were problems of authority when the church started a building project.

- Disunity began when the original person who initiated the vision for the church went away on holiday, returned with a 'prophecy spoken over them' that they are the Pastor of the church and began implementing changes without any communication. [...] was not theologically grounded nor were they willing to submit to anyone.

Theological

- Theological disunity [...] the reason for this is that our sending church was a Pentecostal church. We always had conflicts over salvation because of my Reformed convictions.

- There were some minor theological issues. Our core team was a mix of Charismatics, traditional Evangelicals, and conservative Reformed backgrounds. There was some criticism when certain groups felt we were over-emphasizing something from the 'other' camp.

- We were a rag-bag group of theological positions ...

Sometimes things were positively processed resulting in unity, but that was costly and painful in the early life of a church family:

- There was a lack of clarity about the theological position of the plant early on, but these were worked through to a satisfactory conclusion. Again, though, this cost energy and time.

Relational

- The Core group didn't accept newcomers who were different from them (i.e. the community we were serving) and gossipped about them.'

- Because many of the believers were outcasts, each had baggage or issues between one another. So immediately they had to learn to forgive in a culture of revenge. This led to much disunity.

- Relational disunity with one key couple, who pushed others to leave.

Of course, if disunity within a church plant is crippling, then disunity within a leadership team will be even more so. If you raise up leaders and entrust with power, a 'place at the table', people who are not on the same page as you over the primary issues of vision, theology or ministry philosophy, it's not only exhausting but can be particularly damaging for a young, fragile church which is still getting established.

In their own words:

- I was too generous in appointing people to leadership.

- We were all very compatible, theologically – highly compatible. Relationally, I would say that the leadership was the 'wrong mix.' Too many of our leaders could not be frank or truthful in dealing with uncomfortable situations or in decision making. We made a lot of decisions with which some had serious reservations or even completely disagreed, but didn't express them until after something would crash.

- We weren't clear enough as Elders early on about our working patterns, or how we thought the vision should work out. This meant that there was sometimes tension between us, and confusing signals about the vision were sometimes given to the church.

- A challenge with one leader because he was pursuing a different theological conviction. The other leader left after getting involved in a relationship with another young lady, left to go to a church where there was a pastor he admired. But he also told the church that he was going there because they were serious about discipleship. The problem with that last statement was that we had spent six months working out a discipleship plan for the church – and then he left and everything was halted.

One of the priorities for many planters is to quickly seek to raise up leaders to serve alongside them and share the privilege and responsibility of ministry. I spoke to a couple of planters who were on different sides of the world but had both raised up leaders to an eldership level who, in hindsight, had come with very deliberate agendas in seeking to take the plant in another direction. In both cases these new leaders ended up gathering families and groups from the church around them and seeking to usurp the authority of the original planter. One of these examples ended very painfully, with denominational leaders being called in and indeed eventually removing the planter from their position.

THE SCRIPTURES

The counter cultural unity of the people of God is a significant drumbeat running the length of the New Testament, not simply as a spiritual 'idea' as Christ's death and resurrection in our place forms a new people for Himself, but as a messy, lived, embodied reality, enjoyed within and (even) between local churches. Yet, we can have 'rose-tinted spectacles' about what that unity means – on paper and in theory it sounds nice, but in everyday relationships when people get involved (!), unity is not so easy. The very fact that it is a topic that Paul (and others) need to raise so often, should alert us to this; in simple terms if church unity was easy, they wouldn't need to keep going on about it.

Perhaps it's even more of an issue for a church plant. In the early fragile days when numbers are low and voices can be loud and powerful - the proverbial 'big fish in a small pond'. Or even when a young church can sometimes be seen by other local disgruntled Christians as 'the answer to all my ecclesiological problems' it can be a recipe for a disaster of disunity, as people join expecting perfection, yet bringing along their own imperfections.

One planter put it eloquently when they said:

- A model of 'plant and disaffected Christians will join you' as a growth strategy for planting, still seems to hold sway amongst many local churches.

Consider Paul's letter to the Ephesian church. At the heart of his epistle lies the spiritual truth that the gospel has brought together what sin and rebellion, ever since the Garden of Eden, has blown apart. Into a world of war – both war in the vertical dimension between humanity and God but also the horizontal dimension between humanity and humanity – God has brought peace. Peace even between Jew and Gentile with the dividing wall of hostility being removed and one new humanity constructed. Notice the repetition of the word 'peace' and the resulting household and building that He is constructing:

> For he himself is our peace, who has made the two groups one and has destroyed the barrier, the dividing wall of hostility, by setting aside in his flesh the law with its commands and regulations. His purpose was to create in himself one new humanity out of the two, thus making peace, and in one body to reconcile both of them to God through the cross, by which he put to death their hostility. He came and preached peace to you who were far away and peace to those who were near. For through him we both have access to the Father by one Spirit.
>
> Consequently, you are no longer foreigners and strangers, but fellow citizens with God's people and also members of his household, built on the foundation of the apostles and prophets, with Christ Jesus himself as the chief cornerstone. In him the whole building is joined together and rises to become a holy temple in the Lord. And in him you too are being built together to become a dwelling in which God lives by his Spirit. (Eph. 2:14-22).

This 'household' and 'holy temple' is a glimpse of the future of God's plan when all things are finally united under Christ's Lordship (1:10), but it is also a glimpse into the 'manifold' (or multi-variegated) wisdom of God (3:10). In the Greek version of the Old Testament the root version of the 'manifold' word that Paul uses, is used to describe Joseph's multi-coloured coat. Church was never meant to be mono-tonal but rather, as we are united to Him by faith, so we are united to one another: the breadth of humanity re-united together in local churches.

The problem is, this spiritual fact (what God has done) is often not our lived reality. In churches (and church plants) there can far too frequently be factions, cliques and agendas, power-plays and division. To misquote the traditional marriage service, what God has joined together can often be put asunder. In a world of ongoing, indwelling sin, unity is not natural. That seems to be a large reason why Paul wrote the letter to Ephesus, and it's this truth that shapes the structure of the letter. If the first half (chapters 1-3) outline the glorious theological underpinning of the unity that we now have, the second half (chapters 4-6) works that out in the mess of nitty-gritty, daily relationships. Because of the 'oneness' of our God and the 'oneness' of the church body (4:3-5) so that ought to impact normal church life. Have a look at chapters 4 and 5 especially and you'll see it affects (among other things) how we deal with our anger, our speech and the need to forgive and show compassion when we get it wrong.

The letter ends with a well-known call to don ourselves with gospel armour as we seek to stand firm in the midst of spiritual oppression. Often that's simply taken as a broad reminder that Satan is real and that he sits as our true enemy in life and ministry (and church planting). Which is of course all true. When we consider the context of the letter though and the need to maintain unity, might it be that Paul is reminding them that the spiritual battle they are engaged in, is a battle for unity? Satan loves to divide and disunite what Jesus has reunited through His work on the cross. Yes, of course disunity will be painfully evident because of our own fleshly selfishness, sin and immaturity but ultimately as churches (and church plants) form factions and look increasingly like the world, Satan is smiling.

In Ephesus the underlying problem seems to have been a Gentile/Jew faction. As James wrote a letter 'to the twelve tribes scattered among the nations' he wanted them to guard against a favouritism towards those with money. As Paul wrote to the church in Rome regarding food sacrificed to idols, he urged them to be generous with 'weaker' Christians, (those with tender consciences), urging the 'strong' to use their gospel freedom, not as a means of selfishness, but rather to serve others. The majority serving the minority. Unity mattered to the early church, the body of Christ, and it mattered too to Christ Himself. His final High Priestly prayer in John 17, the night before His death on the cross, was for generations to come who would believe the message of the gospel to be united such that, 'they may be one as we are one—I in them and you in me—so that they may be brought to complete unity. Then the world will know that you sent me and have loved them even as you have loved me.' Of course, in the story of the Bible, perfect 'embodied unity' will not be truly experienced and enjoyed until all the diversity of Christ's people are gathered around His throne. In Revelation John is given a glimpse behind the curtain and records it for us:

> After this I looked, and there before me was a great multitude that no one could count, from every nation, tribe, people and language, standing before the throne and before the Lamb. They were wearing white robes and were holding palm branches in their hands. And they cried out in a loud voice:

> 'Salvation belongs to our God,
> who sits on the throne,
> and to the Lamb.'
> (Rev. 7:9-10)

Until then, in a world of division, for the people of Christ, it's the deliberate, daily decision to live out the unity that Christ has won for us.

SELF-EXAMINATION

These questions can be used for personal reflection, but also can productively be used within a smaller group. Where you see the word 'you' that can work as both a singular and a plural!

1. What issues of church disunity have you personally experienced?

2. Theological? Relational? Vision? Philosophical? Practical? Others?

3. Are there disagreements that you've seen handled well? How about those handled badly? Consider what happened and how you can learn from them.

4. If you were Satan seeking to bring disagreement and disunity to your church plant, what would be your mostly likely strategy?

5. What issues are you willing to 'agree to disagree' over, and what issues are deal-breakers? Do you expect a closer unity on the leadership or staff team? Are there conversations that you need to have with leaders in advance?

6. What practical steps might you take as you go about seeking to deal with disunity in a church? Could you agree and formalise this process in advance to enable healthy expectations among the church plant?

SUCCESSES AND STRATEGIES

We've found that unity in church leadership is everything. Without it elderships and staff teams can't be healthy which means the church won't be healthy. And sadly one of the main reasons why church plants fail, or churches stagnate and close is, because of a lack of unity.

This may seem obvious, but what isn't obvious is that this lack of unity doesn't always manifest itself in ways which we would expect. Disunity in a church could be seen as constant disagreement, elders butting heads, church members' meetings feeling more like the Royal Rumble than an evening of worship and celebration to God's goodness. And all of these are evidence of disunity, but sometimes disunity is because of passive elders not speaking, members not asking questions, people being caught up in 'what God is doing' even when what seems to be accompanying that doesn't sit right – and yet they remain silent.

An answer to the issue of disunity in the church could be 'We have to fight for Unity!' I've heard this many times and it doesn't sit right with me. If we have to fight, who are we fighting? The person who doesn't agree, the people who aren't sure with the direction, the minority? Who are we fighting?

Psalm 133 says that it is good and pleasant when brothers dwell in unity. Notice it doesn't say fight for unity, it says that it is good and pleasant when brothers dwell in unity. When we live in the house of unity that has been built for us by Jesus we don't have to fight for anything or anyone, He has fought that fight, won it, and invited us to dwell in unity with Him and with each other.

The problem we face in church leadership is that we forget that we are living in a house of unity, the question is 'will we dwell in it together, will we live in it?' Because when we live in the unity that Jesus has built, that is good and pleasant, it's how we have been made to function and we will see fruit as God commands a blessing. That means we can disagree, we can question, we can at times part ways in regards to ministry direction, but we do all this whilst still dwelling in unity.

This has been my experience at Cornerstone Church and the Cornerstone Collective here in Liverpool over the past fifteen years of blessed unity because our conviction is that our unity is a given because of the gospel. That means all discussions and decisions flow from that (even the hard ones – and there have been many). Where we do fight, it is to ensure we maintain a culture of dwelling in unity together which makes for space to have robust dialogue over important issues of the church (whatever they may be) and that space is regular – it's times of prayer, times of discussion, it's times of what we call 'mandatory fun' (social time with each other and our wives every month).

Unity in leadership is not about fighting for unity, it's about striving to live in the house of unity that Jesus has built for us and then we lead from that truth.

Steve Robinson
Cornerstone Church, Liverpool

- Appendix 2 lists a number of questions that would help a planting team pre-empt disunity down the line by discussing and agreeing both principle and process from the conception of the plant.

- Helping new people interested in joining your plant to understand where you stand on primary (and secondary) issues of theology and practice is vital. If you plan to have the practice of a formal 'membership', then taking newcomers through classes or studies is especially helpful, particularly those who might be local but coming from different church traditions or backgrounds. It's also important to, where possible, keep gently reminding the church family on where we stand on various issues and why. Don't assume too much!

Further reading for this chapter
- Gavin Ortlund, *Finding the Right Hills to Die On* (Crossway, 2020)
- Mark Deymaz, *Building a Healthy Multi-Ethnic Church* (Jossey-Bass, 2007)

PITFALL 4

🌿 GIFTING 🌿

Planters need to know their strengths and be honest about, and seek help around, their weaknesses

THE STORY

Even from her earliest days Melissa's parents had known she was 'bookish'. She learnt to read from an early age and was usually found with a nose in a book, even when she was supposed to be listening in church. Having aced school she headed for theological training, wanting to serve God on a church staff team or in a parachurch ministry. She thrived. The college library was (almost) her dream come true – books and silence. Following that she was snapped up and recruited by a city centre church, working in an amazingly diverse and dynamic team among undergraduate students. She would have described herself as an introvert, and the team was a bit crazy, but she coped. There were two main universities in town (one near her church in the south of the city, and one a short train ride away in the north) and she had a growing ministry within both of them, meeting with students for Bible studies, reading theological tomes, writing blogs, and supporting the Christian witness on campus as best she could.

She loved time on campus and the discipleship opportunities that student ministry raised, though reading in a coffee shop was, she knew, her sweet spot.

When word of the possibility to plant a campus on the other side of town reached her ears, she jumped at it. The opportunity to be a part of a core team and plant a church that could serve the northern side would be a dream come true.

From her perspective though, it didn't go so well. In the larger church setting, as part of the student team, she could play to her strengths and had people to cover her weaknesses. She had loved to study hard and equip others in her small groups. She had loved her books. Now, as part of the campus staff-team, they had needed her to be out of her comfort zone on the frontline in all kinds of ways; 'flyering' to invite passers-by in town to the new church, chatting to strangers, and welcoming people who visited on a Sunday morning. For an introvert this was a difficult and awkward environment. Their Monday morning staff 'Sunday review' meetings had a similar message week after week, the need to be more welcoming and talk to new people; people loved the service, but were leaving feeling distant. The church began to acquire a reputation of being relationally cold. About a year in she began to wonder if she had made a mistake.

THE STUDY

Quite aside from the prayerful planning, to get a church plant off the ground in the early days takes a huge amount of effort and both an ability and willingness to accomplish a breadth of tasks. The planter needs to be a 'humble generalist'. The 'to-do list' is very long. It may not be that the planter does them all, but someone needs to. The tasks will vary from place to place and context to context, but there will need to be: a capacity to relate well to different types of people and speak of Christ to them; an ability to carefully and appropriately open up the Word of God both to people in the church and guests who arrive; and an ability to deal with administration, fundraising, technical website stuff, and even perhaps social media. Alongside these practical necessities there are fundamental requirements, such as the need to lead the people whom the Lord is sending to you, helping them grasp both the vision of the church, but also the part that they can play to make that vision a reality.

It's all hands on deck in the early stages.

In some models the planter is seen as the one who does all this, the 'all-singing-all-dancing' pastor; in others—and I think that this is preferable—it's shared among the leadership or even the core team. Problems can arise, though, when there are deficiencies within either the planter or the team, and vital tasks are not covered. This idea of not having the right gifts was the most common issue, arising in three-quarters of the examples. It was expressed in words such as ...

- We did not have a team of people who were willing to take on the ministry of the church. We have spent our time ministering to people, and do not have others to help us in that ministry.'

- Mostly stuff I knew before, but now confirmed: I love to preach and feel called to it, but I'm not a community evangelist. I struggle with networking/ getting to know people. I can minister, I think helpfully, to people who are there, but I don't really know how to reach the people who aren't. Personal evangelism in the circle of friends I've built up through the kids' school is okay, but outside a natural context I really struggle.

- In a small church, at least, I need to be able to do a very wide range of things: preach, counsel, organise, design publicity, administer websites ... There is only so much that can be put onto busy lay people. I have the most time, so I do most of the jobs. This doesn't feel like my gifting or my calling, but there just isn't anyone else. So you crack on and do your best.

- I don't think I would plant from scratch again! But if I did, I would have a parent church and a more balanced core team.

Two aspects are vital when it comes to assessing this issue.

1. Know who you are

In a planting culture where we are often inadvertently looking for the omnicompetent individual who is good at everything, it's important to be aware of, and honest about, areas where we're not so strong. There is no shame in this! We are fearfully and wonderfully made. It's okay to be you. In the early days it may be that the planter has to get involved in things they either do not enjoy or are not good at, but over time, ideally, those things ought to be delegated as the size, capacity, and the make-up of the leadership allows. To train and disciple others who can flourish as they exercise their God-given gifts is profoundly rewarding. Many networks encourage candidates to go through a thorough assessment process that will highlight their own strengths and weaknesses which is really helpful.

Some responses highlighted personal gifting weaknesses:

- I'm predominantly gifted in preaching/teaching and leadership. I'm definitely weak in the pastoring/shepherding function.

- I'm not highly gifted as an evangelist, so building a core team as a pioneer is challenging.

- … there is a question whether my gifts have been broad enough to plant. I have had to learn and grow in leadership gifts and people management skills.

- I am not a 'first contact' person by gifting and find the initial stages of relationships difficult. I think the same could be said of most people in the planting team, which is a problem!

- I'm okay at leading a smaller organization, but best at leading a larger organization. I've always known this, but this experience has reinforced that I'm not a shepherd/parish priest. I'm a leader of leaders and strategic visionary.

2. Know who's on your team

Of course, we know we're not looking for the perfect planter, but maybe the wider planting community needs to do more work in patiently recruiting, training, and equipping core teams? Perhaps we need to think with a more holistic team mentality? If we know areas where the key leader is weak then we need to construct a team around them to help them play to their strengths and cover their weaknesses. Core teams are vital, in the sense of assessing the diverse gifts and abilities of the key members of the core team, and in making sure they are well equipped to understand and grasp the vision, and also, crucially, what their role is within that vision. We must avoid 'One-Man-Band' church planting ministries wherever possible. Plants flourish when the planter is comfortable enough to admit their own weaknesses and so to encourage and release others to exercise their own gifts within the body.

THE SCRIPTURES

In chapters 1 and 2 we considered the danger of selecting planters who are gifted, but not godly; competent, but lacking the necessary character. In this section we'll consider some of the gifts or competencies that are actually needed, as well as the importance of a team to complement our deficiencies.

In general terms, Scripture is far more concerned with the pastor's character, than what they can do; however, within the pastoral descriptions for leadership, two key gifts or competencies are highlighted, these ought to be supplemented with a further competency for the role of church planter.

Able to teach

A church elder is to be able to teach (1 Tim. 3:2, Titus 1:9, 2:1 etc). Being able to teach, though, does not necessarily equate to being an amazing orator or charismatic communicator. Rather, it means having a firm grasp of both the gospel and the sound doctrine that flows from it, and being able to teach these things to their people; or, put another way, being able to understand the Bible and convey its meaning. Their teaching can be to individuals, small groups, and to crowds and congregations of varying sizes. As Paul wrote to Titus, most of the churches in Crete were house churches. This sound teaching will be in both more formal contexts (1 Tim. 4) but also in everyday conversation, as well as intentionally seeking to equip others and raise up future generations (2 Tim. 2:2).

Able to reach

Church plants can't simply be a reshuffling of the pack as we move Christians around the map into new church families. Part of our raison d'etre must be the longing to see the gospel shared and taking root and lives transformed. Which means the church planter, perhaps more than a 'normal' pastor, has to be able—along with Timothy (2 Tim. 2:4)—to do the work of an evangelist, and be ready to give a reason for the hope that they have. Church planting is an important means whereby we break new ground and reach new areas. The church plant must be missionally engaged as it reaches out. A church planter needs to have a heart for the lost and an ability to speak to them of Christ.

Able to lead

As we'll cover in the next chapter before being released to lead the household of God, a planter ought to have demonstrated an ability to lead lovingly both themselves and their own households. To do this in a godly manner, the planter will need to possess gifts of Christian leadership, not 'Lording it over as the gentiles do' (Mark 10:42, 1 Pet. 5:3) , but rather laying down their lives for the body in love, helping it not simply to function but to flourish. The leader must be a Christlike example, both leading from within the body but also, as appropriate, leading from the front and calling others to follow.

A vital area of leadership ability is for a planter to enable an often diverse planting team to work well with each other. Paul gives an illustration to help us see how a church body ought to function in 1 Corinthians 12 and Romans 12:3-8:

> For by the grace given me I say to every one of you: Do not think of yourself more highly than you ought, but rather think of yourself with sober judgment, in accordance with the faith God has distributed to each of you. For just as each of us has one body with many members,

and these members do not all have the same function, so in Christ we, though many, form one body, and each member belongs to all the others. We have different gifts, according to the grace given to each of us. If your gift is prophesying, then prophesy in accordance with your faith; if it is serving, then serve; if it is teaching, then teach; if it is to encourage, then give encouragement; if it is giving, then give generously; if it is to lead, do it diligently; if it is to show mercy, do it cheerfully (Rom. 12:3-8).

SELF-EXAMINATION

These questions can be used for personal reflection, but also can productively be used within a smaller group. Where you see the word 'you' that can work as both a singular and a plural!

1. How much of a team player are you? Where do you find it hard to collaborate in leadership? Why? How much do you leave others to lead and how much are you tempted to micromanage different areas of ministry?

2. If you could construct an 'ideal' initial launch leadership team, what gifts would you need to supplement your own? Why?

3. If you could construct an 'ideal' initial core group, what kind of people, with what gifts / experience would you like? Why?

SUCCESSES AND STRATEGIES

Planting churches has revealed that I have been gifted by God in some areas while at the same time exposing a plethora of areas where I have struggled significantly. What I find difficult about that admission is that I can be extremely competent in most aspects that planting requires. I learned sound tech, counselling, liturgies, children's ministry, social media, administration, etc. Planting a church requires that we be more of a utility player who can play multiple positions rather than the star athlete who can focus on the few aspects where they thrive.

When we planted our first church, God sent a couple named Brian and Severine to work with my wife, Jessica, and myself. It was upon meeting Brian that I realized I didn't have what it takes to plant a church that would thrive. I lived in the world of vision and mission. I loved thinking about how the vine of the church would grow and I equipped people to be able to live their normal lives with gospel intentionality. My issue was organising the whole thing. It would have gotten out of control quickly had it not been for God providing another gifted person to come along and carry the full weight of the legal, fiscal, and organisational aspects of the church. It is not an over-exaggeration to say that we would have unintentionally broken many laws regarding non-profits had it not been for Brian.

This has been the story of our church planting journey. God has revealed people who are more gifted and better than I am at different aspects of the church. Each transitional juncture of handing a portion of ministry over to someone else is difficult because I find that I can enjoy almost anything the church needs. But if we are going to keep maturing disciples, multiplying churches, and reaching new people with the gospel, I know that my gifts are going to need to keep moving into the 'new' areas, which constantly requires handing off what I like doing to people who will inevitably be more gifted for that task.

Planting has required me to look around the room for the next gifted person and develop them in order to hand over authority and responsibility. I don't think that will ever change.

Dwight Bernier
Church 21, Montreal, Canada

Further reading for this chapter
- Clint Clifton, *Church Planting Thresholds, A Gospel-Centred Church Planting Guide,* (CreateSpace Independent Publishing Platform 2016).
- Scott Thomas and Tom Wood, *Gospel Coach: Shepherding Leaders to Glorify God* (Zondervan, 2012)

PITFALL 5

🌿 FAMILY ISSUES 🌿

Marriage is hard. Ministry marriages are (possibly) harder, and planting ministry marriages are likely even harder

THE STORY

Looking back they hardly noticed when the drifting began, but it started because of his reluctance to say 'no'. At the beginning he tried to guard the evening slot and only be out for a maximum of three nights each week but as the church began to grow and thrive, in a congregation bustling with busy young professionals, more and more people could only make that time. And so they began to drift. At first it wasn't as if married life was bad, it just wasn't as good. Too often he would arrive home late, and she would be asleep. Too often the previous night's marital niggles were not dealt with, and so they would wake up the next morning starting the day frustrated with each other. Where date night had been a priority, now it had moved down the list and happened perhaps only once each month. And where they had loved just being in each other's company, sharing thoughts and ideas and dreams and prayers, now the time they did have was mostly spent on diary coordination and 'life admin'.

Initially they had been excited about pioneering together to plant the church but, in the end, in part to supplement their funding and make ends meet, she took a part-time job in a local school. They loved her and she loved it. There were opportunities to serve and engage with a number of local families, but it was more than that – she had never really been thrilled about the prospect of being the 'minister's wife' and working in the classroom felt much more like 'her'. It wasn't all plain sailing at the school but he was so taken up with the thriving church she didn't want to burden him with her problems and frustrations. And anyway, he didn't seem to notice anymore when she was down. Like the proverbial frog in the pan of warming water they didn't really notice things were getting dangerously warm until it was almost too late.

She used to joke that he had two wives now; the church and her. But of course it wasn't a joke. Things came to a head one Christmas Eve at the end of a crazy December, when he had just preached at his fourth Carol Service, only to realise he had planned nothing for Christmas for the family. And she said it was 'fine', and 'not to worry' but looking in her eyes, he knew it really wasn't.

The Study

After twenty-five years of marriage, I can confirm that marriage is still complicated! Of course, there's a lot of fun and we love each other, but I'm still too selfish, and my knee-jerk reaction is still far too quickly to think about 'me' and what does this mean for 'me'? There certainly is more of 'we' than 'me', than there used to be. But it's still hard. Our natural bent, this side of eternity will always be towards self.

My wife's granny gave us some advice a few days before our wedding day: 'you'll need to keep forgiving each other, everyday'. She was right. And we do. We are still two unfinished sinners trying to get along. If marriage is hard, ministry marriage can be even harder. Spouses can bear a huge burden, and are often taken for granted, or forever feeling like they're competing with, or losing out to, a new 'woman' in the life of their husband: the church. From the survey and surrounding literature, I wonder if that's even more so in the life of a church planting marriage?

Eighty-three per cent of the planters we spoke to were married, but just over a quarter spoke of significant marital or family strain as a result of planting. From my own experience, planting does put a strain on families for all kinds of reasons: the anxiety of being put out of your depth and your comfort zone in launching a new endeavour, the busyness and hours that are often required, the stress over finances, the bruises from disunity or opposition ... Often, we can be at home in person, but the mind or heart can be elsewhere as we carry the heavy burdens of planting and ministry. Alongside those, however, can be the unhelpful or unnecessary pressures that we can put upon ourselves in seeking to succeed for ungodly or selfish reasons: perhaps proving others wrong, making a name for ourselves and so finding our identity in planting.

One interesting feature of the survey was that many had not been married for very long (an average of ten years) and 87 per cent had young children. What that can mean in everyday practical terms is that life never slows down: the busyness of planting a church through the day is sandwiched either side with a busy home life; nappies to be changed, night fears to be calmed, school lunches to be prepared, skinned knees to be cleaned and plastered, bath times to be supervised, bedtime stories to be read, and dishwashers to be emptied and filled. And then repeat. And repeat. Outside the home, the church family or co-leaders may not be aware of it, but at home and behind closed doors, the stories show that planting life can be very painful and raw. As we saw in chapter four, no doubt there is a spiritual element to this too, with the reality that Satan loves to target and divide – not just church families, but Christian family units as well.

Have a listen to some of the voices from the study. Notice that one experienced pastor comments on the added strain that planting has placed upon their marriage, a strain that wasn't there in previous ministry. Notice also the added strain reported by a lead planter and his wife, who came to feel that they had sacrificed so much for the plant that it had become a trap that they felt unable to walk away from if things didn't work out:

- Church planting is very hard work. I have to deny my family time to be on the field doing the work of church planting.

- My children are not able to go to a good school and so we had to put them in a school which we could afford but did not offer good education. We had to do extra work to make sure that we added on to what they were being given.

- This plant has been immensely hard on our marriage from the inside. I'd say my wife and I are weary of the difficulties that planting has brought out, which weren't evident through all my other years of pastoring.

- If you have small cracks in your marriage, those cracks will become large crevasses that will cause large divides in your relationship. Work hard on your marriage before you plant, as you plant, and don't stop! Don't lose your wife or your family to your church plant.

- Planting put a huge amount of pressure on our marriage. We often describe the additional pressure of planting with the idea that if it goes wrong, everyone else gets to walk away but us. The church was paying my salary and therefore our mortgage. We had spent our savings on building a garden room at the bottom of our garden, which, while necessary for us, also contained [the] Church's office space. We had little to no reserves and so when the church looked like it would fail, which happened more regularly than we were comfortable with, it put a huge amount of pressure on our marriage. That resulted in bitterness and hurt and also created a bit of a vicious cycle as it made it hard for us to show the hospitality that we needed for the church to grow.

Some reported that their marriages had been left significantly weakened through the experience, and even that some couples have been forced to leave the project for the sake of the relationship:

- Our marriage didn't impact the planting experience, but the experience greatly impacted our marriage. We left as broken shells of what we had been. Our marriage was in ruins.

- I worked too much and didn't take adequate breaks. I felt guilty when we would rest, but my wife needed time out of the isolation and rugged living conditions. The ministry was my mistress for many of those years. Many difficult and dangerous situations came our way, causing PTSD and triggering my wife. I did not care or help in these situations, in fact I often made matters worse. Our marriage is solid now because, in the end, I left that ministry so we could heal as a family.'

Other respondents left sage advice ...

- Love Jesus, your wife, and your kids more than you love the idea/process of planting.

- Do not sign up with any organization/network that does not have support, training and coaching for both spouses. Ask to see their finances and what they spend on training and support and how it's divvied out for both spouses.

- Attend a solid and well recommended assessment where both spouses are required to attend.

- Regardless of whether you are the planter or the spouse, church planting will deeply impact your life. This has been found to be true in all cultures and contexts. So know what you are getting into. Research it. Interview planting couples about it. Be sure both husband and wife do due diligence before you set out on this path.

THE SCRIPTURES

The personal cost of church planting absorbed by the planter's family—whatever the model employed—means that a household with underlying divisions is on shaky ground. The planter's spouse, but also any children, need to be helped, prepared, and equipped for the reality of the project. In the two main passages listing qualities for eldership in the pastoral epistles, an elder/overseer is called to be one who lovingly serves and leads their family well.

- An elder must be blameless, faithful to his wife, a man whose children believe and are not open to the charge of being wild and disobedient (Titus 1:6).

- Now the overseer is to be above reproach, faithful to his wife, temperate, self-controlled, respectable, hospitable, able to teach, not given to drunkenness, not violent but gentle, not quarrelsome, not a lover of money. He must manage his own family well and see that his children obey him, and he must do so in a manner worthy of full respect (1 Tim. 3:2-4).

Paul is not demanding perfection, but part of his point is that if an elder/overseer is unable to lovingly lead their own family in a way that brings unity and maturity, they ought not be seeking to lead the family of God. A largely harmonious house is a prerequisite for pastoral ministry. The gifts, the skills, and the strategies needed to pastor a family in all its complexity (and mess), is a training arena for local church ministry. Again, it's right to reiterate that perfection is not the necessary standard (what family is perfect?!). The supermarket temper tantrums, the yelling and door slamming of the teenager, or even the awkwardness and arguments between husband and wife do not disqualify a pastor from ministry. However, if there is significant disagreement between a husband and wife regarding a desire to church plant then particular care and caution ought to be exercised. The all-in, costly nature of planting (perhaps especially a 'parachute' plant into a new area) will exacerbate pre-existing cracks and tensions.

SELF-EXAMINATION

These questions can be used for personal reflection, but also can productively be used within a smaller group. Where you see the word 'you' that can work as both a singular and a plural!

1. On a scale of 1-10, if you're married, how supportive is your spouse of this church plant? What does your

spouse see their role as? What will (and won't) they be involved in?

2. How can you practically make sure ministry does not become more important to you than your spouse? What regular opportunities can you put in place to communicate honestly with your spouse? Or vice versa.

3. If you're a parent, how will you prioritise your children? How will you model the joy of gospel service to your family?

SUCCESSES AND STRATEGIES

When we read about church planting and spoke to those who had already planted, we saw that hospitality and socialising were not just fun but essential. We have enjoyed throwing our lives into this. However, we have recognised a tendency sometimes to do too much and get emotionally tired. We identified some signs that our pace was getting a bit much for us.

We realised it was better to preserve our family than fulfil the model church planting amount of socialising and hosting. Therefore, we have reduced what we do for this season and will be careful about adding more. We have also started a weekly scheduling meeting to review what is coming up in the future days, weeks and months.

Preaching on Genesis 2:1-3 was helpful too. I realised that I worked hard Sunday to Friday for the Church, then on Saturday, if we were not socialising, I worked hard in my home doing DIY and chores. We seldom just stopped and enjoyed each other as a family for a full day. Since then, I've tried to factor in time during the week for household jobs and DIY so that my day off is a family-focused rest.'

Kenny & Lesley Rogan
Hope Church Aviemore, UK

Further reading and resources for this chapter

- Tim Keller, *The Meaning of Marriage* (Hodder & Stoughton, 2013)
- Christine Hoover, *The Church Planting Wife* (Moody Publishers, 2013)
- Parakaleo is a ministry exclusively for the support of wives in church planting. It's based in the US in New York but has an increasingly global reach: https://www.parakaleo.us

PITFALL 6

✹ PRIORITY ✹

Planters can drift into trusting things other than the gospel to bear fruit

THE STORY

On paper, the core team had every conceivable base covered. Someone to do all the design, website, and printing, an incredibly gifted musician who moonlighted in a local band, a treasurer who felt (possibly too) comfortable spending time in excel, people with pastoral counselling training, talented youth and children's workers as well as project managers, logistics experts, and even someone who worked in risk-assessment! Part of the main challenge for the planter was going to be the task of seeking to coordinate this extraordinary bunch, but there was a confidence that with this team nothing could really go wrong.

As the church began things started off well. The 'soft-launch' ironed out a few glitches and a good turnout for the public launch service meant everyone left feeling really challenged by a powerful message. They moved from there into a Sunday series from Proverbs outlining different aspects of wise and godly living, and their small groups tracked with the same passages for further depth and application.

It was a busy church but the different parts of the 'machine' worked well together. Week by week, everyone grew in understanding of how their faith was to affect different areas of life.

About six months in, the pastor was at a biblical counselling conference, and, as he drove back reflecting on what he had heard, he felt a curious mix of emotions: joy, but also unease. He didn't have a list of things to do or to implement or work through—the main speaker at the conference had simply expounded the glories of God's kindness and graciousness. Driving home, he had a feeling of security, comfort, and a heart full to bursting with praise. So, why did he feel uneasy? As he drove down the motorway he realised it was because so often his own aim in preaching was to send his congregation away feeling challenged. He knew of all kinds of pastoral problems in the church, all kinds of half-heartedness, and so the forty minute pulpit opportunity each week was his chance to seek to put right some of these issues. He kind of liked being known as 'a challenging preacher'. And yet there was very little joy in the church – just a lot of busyness and a lot of hard work.

THE STUDY

One of the complicated truths that we've already seen is that for many planters there is a real tension between the desire for the plant to thrive quickly (to justify funding, investment, etc.), and the fact that God's timescale often does not match our own. Seeds take time to grow. Fruit is not always immediately evident. With Him, a day is like a thousand years, and a thousand years are like a day! (2 Pet. 3:8). God is not in a rush. Mix that in with the quick-fix-fast-moving nature of our impatient society and the fact that planters are often young and inexperienced (44 per cent from the study were under thirty-six), and you end up with a painfully steep learning curve over the need for patience. Many naively went in expecting quick results, but learnt the hard way that this is not the norm (more on that in the next chapter).

Have a listen to some examples when asked about what they had learnt about planting:

- It's really, really, really slow. People (including me!) change slowly, and I can do nothing to hurry it on, apart from encourage and pray.

- Church ministry is often slow – take time to savour the fruit that comes – particularly the steady growth in people's lives.

- It really is often thankless work and you have to take the long view.

- It's not about what we can see, but trusting in what God is doing behind the veil.

- I get down too easily and lose sight of God's eternal plan. I'm too quick to give in to resentment when people say they are committed and aren't. I'm not prayerful enough. I want quick fixes and lack patience.

Alongside that patience, there developed, for a number, a greater clarity and focus on what priorities ought to shape a ministry that builds for the long-term. What tasks ought to be at the very top of the planter's to-do list each week? What concerns need to make their way into the diary first?

Strikingly, rather than any 'quick-fix, how-to, silver-bullet' guides that can be so attractive to some, or indeed a 'generalist-activism' that can often shape the early years of a plant (see chapter four), for a number of planters there came a clearer resolve to simplicity in ministry; to prioritise the Bible and prayer.

Again, have a listen to their own words when planters were asked what they learnt regarding church ministry:

- You're no one's saviour as a planter, nor are you first and foremost a planter—you are a beloved child of the Father no matter what happens in your plant. You are not the saviour ... You are pointing to the Saviour[?]. Do the Lord's work in the Lord's Way, (see Francis Schaeffer's article of same name).

- It's hard. Things happen really slowly. There's very little feedback. It relies a lot on prayer ... the Word is powerful. You need people you can rely on, train up and delegate to. You need people who will tell you that you are wrong.

- Let the Word do the work. That's my phrase—that many use—and it's the truth. We want to build God's church through His Word. Not just through preaching, but in every way. God does build His church that way ...

- Church isn't about one-on-one personal discipleship, it's first and foremost about Word and Sacraments and prayer.

- Personally, I care less about production quality than I did before. For example, lighting and staging matters even less than I thought and we already run quite simple.

A friend, Reuben Hunter, who's written helpfully on this idea reduces this down to three necessary elements: discipline, humility, and faith.

Discipline

When you get started, particularly if you are planting from scratch, if something is going to get done you will need to be the guy who does it. And there are literally hundreds of things you could do. Fund raising, meeting people, website, social media, community involvement, organising venues, musicians, song words, Sunday school materials, signage, coffee. All very good and very important things, but they need to find their place beneath your careful study and proclamation of the Word of God.

Humility

There are lots of things you could give time to in planting a church that will get you a pat on the back, virtually no one will praise you for preaching or teaching the Bible.

And faith

The Lord Jesus Christ has promised to build His church. And He does this through the preaching of the Word of God.[1]

The mantra 'What you win them with is what you win them to' is common in church leadership circles, and, in our survey, it seemed to be a lesson that a number of struggling planters had been forced to grasp. For healthy growth the flashy and exciting strategies did not create long-term maturity, but rather a quick crowd who were easily distracted by other things when offered by other people.

THE SCRIPTURES
God creates by speaking

Whereas we use hands or tools, He uses words. Just as God created at the beginning in Genesis 1 through a word, so

---

1. Reuben Hunter, 'Method: Word-centred church planting', in *Multiplying Churches, Exploring God's Mission Strategy,* ed. Steve Timmis, (CFP, 2016), 100.

now He recreates through words, bringing life to our dead hearts and light into our darkness. As He took on flesh at the incarnation, so came The Word, with words, bringing order out of chaos, transformation out of suffering, joy out of tears, life out of death.

At the beginning we threw off what we thought were the restrictive shackles of God's words, distrusting His character and His goodness, and subsequently we were scattered in judgment. Now we are in Christ, gathered again as the people of God, built on the foundation of the apostles, prophets, evangelists, pastors, and teachers (Eph. 4:11): different and distinct, yet united as gifts of word ministry. God bringing light and life once again, recreating us into His image. Through His Word, God equips His people for works of service, bringing maturity, bringing life.

In the Bible, whenever the people of God gather together they do so around His Word, and so we should not be surprised at the way in which Paul highlights and prioritises the teaching and preaching of the Word of God, both in his own ministry and in the ministries of those in whom he will invest for the sake of future generations.

Think of his relationship with Timothy, and his concern for him to particularly prioritise teaching through the pastoral epistles for those in church leadership (1 Tim 3:2, 4:11-14, 5:17, 2 Tim 1:13, 2:2,24, 3:10,16 and Titus 2). Paul is clear that the key priority for the gospel minister must be that of teaching, both at a weekly gathering, but also investing in individuals. God's Word is to be at the heart of a church body.

Another place where this is especially clear is in chapter two of Paul's first letter to the Thessalonians. The apostle faced hardship and opposition in Thessalonica, but, despite that, he pressed on and persevered in proclaiming the gospel. Here we see both Paul's motives for sharing the gospel with them, but also the model by which he did so. Like a mother, he lovingly cared for them and shared his life with them, and like a father he urged them on to live lives worthy of the kingdom of God. And their response? By the Spirit, they accepted it not simply as a human word, 'but as it actually is, the word of God, which is indeed at work in you who believe' (1 Thess. 2:13).

The danger in the world of church planting is that you can be steered off course by either the promises of silver bullets that will make your church plant thrive or by the length of your to-do list, resulting in sermon prep and time in the Word being sidelined. The simple truth is that there is no silver bullet: no website, strategy, programme, methodology, human book (not even one claiming to give you twelve reasons why church plants struggle!), or marketing package that will make your church thrive. God grows His church. And He grows it through the careful, prayerful preaching and teaching of His Spirit-exhaled Word. It's there, as we open up the Scriptures verse by verse, paragraph by paragraph, book by book, that He powerfully speaks, transforms and grows His people in maturity, bringing life to our dead hearts, light into our darkness.

So, don't get distracted. It's very easy. Our hearts, like moths around a flickering bulb, love novelty and new ideas. But, if I may echo Paul's words to Timothy,

> In the presence of God and of Christ Jesus, who will judge the living and the dead, and in view of his appearing and his kingdom, I give you this charge: Preach the word; be prepared in season and out of season; correct, rebuke and encourage—with great patience and careful instruction (2 Tim. 4:1-2).

SELF-EXAMINATION
These questions can be used for personal reflection, but also can productively be used within a smaller group. Where you see the word 'you' that can work as both a singular and a plural!

1. Where are you tempted to find assurance in something other than God's grace? What are your 'nightmares' and your 'daydreams'? What do they reveal about you and your heart?

2. What might a sermon or Bible study look like that is not founded upon grace?

3. What temptations do you feel to seek to grow the church through something other than the Word of God?

SUCCESSES AND STRATEGIES

Planting a church is hard work. Vision needs to be shared. Teams need to be developed. Members need to be pastored. People need to be evangelised. Leaders need to be trained. Structures need to be established. Money needs to be raised. Buildings need to be found. Sermons need to be preached. Websites need to be built. Social media accounts need to be managed. Books need to be read. Conferences need to be attended. The list could go on and on because planting a church involves a to-do-list the length of your arm and then some.

But there I was, three years into planting Living Hope, spending yet another day just lying on my couch. Through a mysterious hip injury, God put me on my back for six weeks so that I was unable to tick anything off my significant to-do-list. For that, I couldn't be more grateful to Him. Through that time God helped me to see that I had stopped trusting in Him and started trusting in myself to plant this church. At some point in the season while planting a church, I'd started to believe that I would build my church.

I felt like the future of Living Hope depended on what I could do. Wrongly thinking that our church would grow if I could share the vision compellingly enough, preach sermons powerfully enough, welcome people warmly enough, care for members deeply enough, run programmes that were attractive enough, evangelise the community effectively enough, develop an online presence that was engaging enough and get onto the next ministry strategy early enough.

So I'm grateful to God that, in His kindness, He put me on the couch and opened my eyes to my pride and foolishness. While I lay down, He built our church up. The church grew as members used gifts in ways that they wouldn't have been able to if I'd been there. Sermons were preached, people were welcomed, members were cared for, programmes were run, the community was evangelised and new people joined, all while I sat on my couch. It turns out that I wasn't as important as I thought I was!

While on my couch, God helped me to stop believing the lie that I would build my church and start trusting Jesus' promise that He will build His church. What a relief it is to know that.

While church planting is still hard work and I still have a to-do-list the length of my arm, I now do my work while resting in the promise that the future of Living Hope doesn't depend on me and what I can do, it depends on Jesus and what He will do. For that I'm so grateful!

Pete Rennie
Living Hope Church, Inverness, Scotland

Further reading resources for this chapter
- William Still, *The Work of the Pastor* (Christian Focus Publications, 2010)
- Peter Brain, *Going the Distance* (Matthias Media, 2006)
- J. I. Packer, *Evangelism and the Sovereignty of God* (IVP, 2010)

Six External Pitfalls Outside the Church Plant

PITFALL 7

❧ PLANTING CULTURE ❧

We must make it okay for people to talk about their struggles

THE STORY

Over the years he had learned to hide quite how competitive he was. A straight A's student at school, but quiet about it; able to just blend in. Outwardly he seemed humble and self-effacing, inwardly he was fiercely proud. He set himself high standards which meant not getting the marks he hoped for in a test or an essay would result in him beating himself up for the next few days and doubling down to do even better next time.

When he graduated (with distinction) from seminary and was scooped up by his placement church with the task of planting a new congregation on the other side of town, he again said the right kind of things about expectations and hopes for growth, but inside he had no doubt that the plant would thrive. He knew it would be hard work, but had devoured the papers and case studies and calculated the formula for growth. They were starting with fifty, but by the end of the first year hoped to be 100, by year three expected to be at 400, and by the end of year five they would be pushing 1000 as well as planning to plant their first congregation. What could go wrong? There was a guy in the next city over who had started something similar and seen incredible growth; all kinds of Christians and 'Prodigals' had come out of the woodwork and joined his plant.

He would catch himself daydreaming about being asked to speak at the big conferences and share his thoughts on why his church had done so well.

Launch day happened with a core of fifty-five (more than expected – he wasn't surprised), and then over the coming months church life 'began' as the various plans and programmes kicked in. Invitations were (beautifully) designed, printed, and distributed, doors were opened, and people... trickled in. What was happening? Where was the tidal wave? The team had done their research in advance and knew what the local area needed. Had the invites gone out? What was happening?

Over the coming months a few people did come and try the church out, and a few stayed. But by the end of the first year they weren't 100 – they were actually only forty-five. A number of core team members had been forced to move for work reasons and others had hoped the daughter church wouldn't be quite so much like the mother church. It was a similar story as the years progressed, with a few joining each year and a few moving on or away; by year three they were sixty and by year five they were only eighty-five. The mother church had stuck by them, though at year three had decided to stop providing so much funding because the plant didn't seem to be a good investment for an organisation with a tight budget.

The church is still meeting, but only just about limping along. Often he wonders what he did wrong and why things haven't grown as they should have. Why had the church in the neighbouring town flourished and not his? He had dreamed of a church that was significant and big and would impact this side of town for the gospel but ended up with a small congregation of people who were really not world-changers.

THE STUDY

As I began to process and present some of the results of the study, one seminary student fed back their appreciation - describing plant failure as a 'taboo subject – just not something we really talk about'. This was not an uncommon thread within both the responses and wider literature. We only really hear of the successes. Until I began to do some further research and reading for this, I had never heard of anyone who had been given a platform or a pulpit to talk about how their church plant had gone wrong, and to be honest the examples I did find were very rare. It takes a humble planter to be willing to vulnerably and honestly speak of how things hadn't turned out as they had prayed and planned. And a brave network to give them the opportunity to do it.

Church planters (having been there personally) can be an insecure bunch. We're experts at taking our photographs of the new church gatherings so it looks like the room is fuller than it really is. We're prone to slight 'strutting', rounding up the numbers, and a little exaggeration. We idolise and devour the autobiographies and strategies of those who are 'killing it'. We love to hear stories of funding secured, of growing attendance figures, of baptism numbers, of targets met, of planting teams sent, of movements started, of networks thriving. It turns out though, if you dig a bit deeper, more plants struggle than we might expect. We just don't often hear about them.

This ties in with the point made by the previous chapter. We're a people who, on paper, know it's all about grace, but we're not great at admitting (in detail at least) the reality — our fears, failures, and frustrations; our disappointments and disasters. It's as if, in practice, we veer towards seeking to justify ourselves by our works, longing to be seen as a successful church planter (whether in pastoring a large church or planting a number of smaller churches). Trouble is, if you do that and if I do that, then the culture that we're a part of (and so we help to create) means everyone only hears about the good news stories. It's something that much of the literature picks up on; Clifton in Church Planting Thresholds[1] speaks of the danger of platforming the superstar model as our paradigm for planting, whilst Bennardo in his book suggests that, rather than raising up the 'lottery winners', at church planting conferences we should, 'elevate, celebrate, and make room on the main platform for the long-term, faithful veterans with a reputation for retaining healthy environments and staying on task'.[2]

The trouble is that if the planting scene is dominated by a culture that says no one fails, then church planters will believe that we won't (or can't) fail. This will lead to a belief that everyone else is doing fine when we are struggling. Many responders reported something similar to this particular kind of naivety: they began with unhelpfully hopeful expectations of where their plant might be in three years' time and beyond.

In their own words:

> • This planting 'failure' is masked from the wider world. There's a significant inconsistency in how we're speaking about ourselves here, and how [my planting network] understands us to be. So no one in [our planting network] would have thought to ask the question [of how they can help].

---

1. Clifton, *Church Planting Thresholds: A Gospel-Centered Guide*, p.3.
2. Bennardo, *The Honest Guide to Church Planting,* p. 103.

- The books make it sexy; the reality is it is so hard.

- Planting in an unreached area – an urban secular area like [ours] will take longer than you think.

- ... when I planted a missionary friend told me within a year 500 people will be members at Mission ... and nothing but the opposite has happened. I once said this would be the most difficult thing I do in ministry ... and it has been.

One of the questions we asked of people was what they would do differently if they were to plant again, or if they were to advise and coach future planting generations. A number spoke of more patience and (as we touched on in chapter 2 and 6) better pacing:

- ... I would start much slower and not launch on a Sunday straight away. I would also make sure I took longer to build a bigger, stronger team ...

- Set expectations more realistically. Don't worry about launching quite so soon. Ask for more commitment from the core team.

- Slower than before and away from the pressure to perform.

- Begin with a larger core team, stronger leadership group, more diversity of giftings. Take things slower – work, plan and strategise towards a twenty-year vision not just getting things off the ground.

In hindsight, I wonder if one of the reasons people were reticent to take part in this project boiled down to a sense of shame. 'Conference comparisons' can be crippling. People feel they've failed (because they never hear of the struggles of others) and think they're the only ones who have found it hard.

Anecdotally, in a conversation with one of the directors of training from the Redeemer City to City Network in New York as we were designing the study questions, he advised that, at least in the US, it would likely be a struggle to find people willing to talk, because many leave the ministry if a plant doesn't work out. The crushing shame and sadness that 'failed' planters felt, resulted in them entirely changing their life trajectory.

Now, only 26 per cent of those pastor/planters we spoke to were not in a paid Christian-ministry capacity anymore. Some were working in non-profits, some had retired, and some were still looking for what the Lord would have them do. What's clear though in having had the privilege of reading responses, is that those who have been through hardships have much to teach the rest of us. Rather than this disqualifying someone from future ministry, we should be more willing to see them as qualified: a hugely important resource to learn from and invest in the next generation. Indeed, having learnt valuable lessons, a number had gone on, to plant other churches. I was also encouraged that others had been hired to help oversee and coach younger planters:

- After almost two years of being in no-man's land we are now serving a church part-time and I have started coaching pastors and church planters.

- Yes – I am now a field director overseeing 70+ missionaries including a number of church plants.

THE SCRIPTURES

The gospel of the Lord Jesus ought to redefine the way that we think about leadership.

The humility and example of Christ as our model for leadership is a rich theme to explore through the Scriptures, perhaps particularly for the context of strong pioneering church planters. He is the One who came not to be served but to serve and to give up His life as a ransom for many (Mark 10:45). He is the One who did not consider equality with God something to be grasped but rather took on flesh and made Himself a servant, dying a cursed death for His people (Phil. 2:5-11). However, Paul's letters to the Corinthian church, and especially his second letter, give us helpful light and insight into the dangers of unhealthy ideas about leadership.

When Paul wrote to the Christians in Corinth, no one's entirely sure exactly who he has to defend his ministry to, but it's clear that, whoever they were, they believed Christian leaders ought to be forceful, eloquent and impressive. They delight in highlighting that Paul was not like that, and so could not be taken seriously. To be impressive in their eyes, you had to look impressive. The trouble is that their understanding of leadership had far more to do with Corinth than with Christ. Our world is still painfully Corinthian, and so the danger can be that our model of church planting leadership can also sound very ... Corinthian; we don't hear much about where projects don't go as planned or simply don't work. The church planting conference speakers can often seem very impressive, asked to speak because they are 'getting it right'. And yet as Paul defends himself and his ministry, he carefully unpicks their wrong thinking, showing both why Corinthian leadership is unhelpful, but helping us to see why, as he points us to Christ.

Where Corinth loved rhetoric and oratory skills, Paul happily arrived on the scene not with,

… eloquence or human wisdom as I proclaimed to you the testimony about God. For I resolved to know nothing while I was with you except Jesus Christ and him crucified. I came to you in weakness with great fear and trembling. My message and my preaching were not with wise and persuasive words, but with a demonstration of the Spirit's power, so that your faith might not rest on human wisdom, but on God's power (1 Cor. 2:1-5).

Where these 'super-apostles' (2 Cor. 11:5) sought to project an image of strength and power, Paul was very happy to be open about his weakness (such that he is labelled by them as 'unimpressive' and a fool (2 Cor. 10:10, 11:16)). Paul knows that he follows a King who wore a crown of thorns and was mocked and ridiculed and yet was glorified in His suffering. Paul knows that the gospel of the suffering servant redefines what we believe about leadership.

Where they downplayed or airbrushed the reality of suffering, Paul is happy to talk about his own sharing in the sufferings of Christ (2 Cor. 1:5). More than this, he is happy to talk about the comfort he draws from this reality. Indeed, as we've already seen (back in chapter 1) it's often through our suffering and hardships that God draws us to Himself, and so we are forced to rely, not upon our own gifts and abilities, but upon Him (2 Cor. 12). Indeed, perhaps, like Paul, our loving Father gives us a perpetual thorn that weakens us and so reminds us that He is enough.

Of course, this doesn't mean that we should not work hard on our sermons or leadership, or that we should go looking for suffering, but it does mean we ought to both take care in our own leadership model and values, but also in the image that we project to others. If we're inadvertently projecting or collectively elevating the kind of message that implies we've got it all together, that will easily create a culture of success where problems and weakness are seen as abnormal. It's then that church planting culture slides into appearing to be Corinthian.

SELF-EXAMINATION

These questions can be used for personal reflection, but also can productively be used within a smaller group. Where you see the word 'you' that can work as both a singular and a plural!

1. Have you ever spoken in depth to a church planter who has struggled significantly? What did you learn? How will their experience shape your methodology?

2. Why do you think we generally don't hear much about plants that don't go well?

3. How will you feel if things don't go well?

4. How can you be appropriately honest about your struggles and failures?

SUCCESSES AND STRATEGIES

We planted the church expecting massive growth in one year but we have since realized that our expectation was based on wrong assumptions. The majority of people in Gulu do not believe so much in a church that exposes the gospel message. They need churches that preach prosperity and how God is going to make them overcome their current problems.

We launched the church on the 1st of May 2022 with 130 adults and 60 children attending our worship gathering for the first two months, but when they realized there was no material benefit they were getting from this new church plant, many decided to leave and went back to those churches that preach what they wanted to hear. Our expectation was that after our one year anniversary we would be having massive growth in numbers even as the church members grew spiritually.

We received another setback in April 2023 when the owner of the hotel we launched our church services from asked the church to leave his hotel. He told us that the manager made a mistake to allow the church to meet in his hotel conference room. We lost some people in the process of relocating to a new venue. Our expectation of the speed of growth has been met with frustration and discouragement along the way. We have since retreated to a place of prayer and weekly evangelism so that we can reach new people who might be obedient to follow Christ faithfully. In the last two weeks, we managed to get four new believers whom we are currently discipling as we trust that they will mature to also disciple others.

We have since discovered that we must rely on the Holy Spirit fully for any step that we will take to see the growth and expansion of God's Kingdom here in Gulu and Northern Uganda.

Richard Okello
Seven Mile Road Church, Gulu, Uganda

Planting in rural Ireland has been described as attempting to plough granite. With few churches, fewer resources, and many centuries of history, beginning a planting journey often involves a long-term investment rather than a short-term explosion. As we began our planting journey we realised very early on that sometimes standing still was progress. Of course this isn't an easy thing to come to terms with. As the days, weeks, and months ticked by the urge to see movement, growth and excitement often led us to discouragement.

The challenges for church planters can fall into two categories; competitiveness and comparison. With the scarcity of churches in our region, we would fall into comparison as we saw the growth of other plants, the videos of joyful faces, the social media posts that caused us to question if we were the right people, or were doing things in the right way. Having peers in similar contexts, and mentors to give us perspective, we were able to look beyond 'growth' as an external increase, but to see it as rather a 'depth' to press into. Furthermore, to realise that God had placed others around us in our plant to be on this journey with us. My wife would often remind us both that we are in a marathon, not a sprint. That keeping our eyes on the next marker ahead rather than longing for a finish line would help us to focus on those we were running with. All of a sudden the plodding became plodding together with our church family. The words of self-doubt became words of shared encouragement. The bursts of energy as the winds of God's grace drove us on helped us celebrate and rejoice. As one of our church members would regularly say with a wink, 'It's almost as if God knows what He's doing!' Sometimes in those slow seasons, I need to remind myself of this, find peace in it, and trust Him for each slow step onward.

Jonny Pollock
Loughrea, Co. Galway. Ireland

Further reading and resources for this chapter

- Jason Helopoulous, *The New Pastor's Handbook: Help and Encouragement for the First Years of Ministry* (Baker Books, 2015)
- John James and Neil Powell, *Together for the City – How Collaborative Church Planting Leads to Citywide Movements* (IVP, 2019)

PITFALL 8

❧ STRATEGY ❧

Rather than a copy and paste top-down approach, plants must think strategically and intentionally at ground-level

THE STORY

The request had come from the head office of his church planting network that they really needed a plant in that part of that city. It was strategic. If the bright young students and professionals living and working there could be reached, then they could be deployed around the world to plant other churches for their network. He had spoken to friends within his local fraternal about it, and they had pointed out that the area was already pretty saturated with churches; it seemed that every denomination, stream, and network had had a similar idea—to reach, build, and send within that place. When this objection was raised at his own church, however, people would respond by arguing that 'there are more than enough unbelievers to go around', and these unbelievers were really worth pouring out resources to reach.

To the folks at head office it had great potential: money, people, and resources would be liberally thrown behind it and it would be platformed wherever possible. He felt an extraordinary sense of privilege, pride, and responsibility to be called to serve his tribe in this way. Following a meeting to hear their vision, he left with the understanding that, essentially, the next three decades depended upon churches reaching out to, and raising up leaders that could then be trained and deployed for the years to come.

As promised, money, people, and resources were generously provided and while there were—sort of—'more than enough unbelievers to go round,' he hated the feeling of 'competition'. The reality was that through the Autumn term there would be a scramble to see if some students and new professionals might settle with you. Very few did. And those that did, didn't really help much with finances or helping the church to become self-sufficient. Being asked to plant was a huge privilege, but he really felt the pressure to grow and succeed, eyes were on them, time was ticking. Some of their key funders and supporters expected measurable results, and they expected them soon.

The denominational leaders were patient and their regular catch-ups were warm, but in a city where there were a huge number of small- and medium-sized churches representing almost every stream and 'brand' you can think of, each seeking to scoop a slice of the pie, each paying huge amounts of weekly rent for a hall near the local university, none really thrived. In fact, over time he began to realise that they came and went fairly regularly. It was a treadmill: one church would leave, exhausted and weary and broken, and another, full of hope, energy and vision, would arrive.

His turn to leave came when the funding dried up after four years. He was drained and disillusioned, and eventually took a job on staff at a larger church.

THE STUDY
Church planting is mushrooming all over the world. Things may have slowed during the pandemic, but once again

denominations and networks are seeking to plant healthy churches which will go on and reproduce and plant more and more churches. That's a really good thing – we need more and more church communities, shaped by the gospel, holding out the hope of Christ, bringing light to a dark world. However, as with the scenario above, our survey revealed a common problem: a network or denomination seeking to plant a church in a locality, but with very little by way of local knowledge. Perhaps the plant was seen as strategic? Perhaps (at my most cynical) the network or denomination wanted to raise its own flag in that part of that town.

There are a number of problems with this kind of methodology. Unless it's done sensitively, the new plant can very easily feel like the vision is being imposed upon it. Rather than a local church to reach these people in this place, it can feel more like this new plant exists only as part of a wider plan for a denominational strategy. It almost seems like it ought to go without saying, but a local church should exist primarily for its local area. And, as we'll see more in chapter ten, we need to understand the context of an area well, before we seek to plant within it.

- This was a plant by remote control. Planted by people, who, whilst living in the area, did not represent the area.

- We probably could have explained the VISION of our mission board better.

- It's not difficult to build a crowd in big cities, but I don't really like the 'flagship' strategic concept ... rather than seeking to become a church of 500 we've decided to be generous and invest in world mission ...

Another negative outcome of the 'strategic church plant imposed from above' can be those areas or regions we tend to see as 'strategic' end up being saturated with church plants. This, in turn, can be detrimental to the churches already established, or to other plants seeking to take root.

One striking example of this was a planter in Australia whose urban church plant lasted for eight years and bore much fruit. However, within that eight years he informed me one of the reasons they continually struggled was that they were 'haemorrhaging' people as members of his church were attracted to other newer church plants, offering 'better' ministries. He then clarified that, within their district of approximately 15,000 people, no less than thirty-eight (!) plants had come and gone in that period. Of those thirty-eight, roughly twenty were plants from overseas. His indigenous church plant was weakened in large part due to denominations from overseas seeking to start another church within their town.

The Australian example is very helpful in highlighting the danger of church planting without communication, or indeed perhaps collaboration. When everyone is seeking to reach the same area, maybe for legitimate reasons, the plants can be detrimental to one another. Like two goldfish in a tank, where each secretes hormones to limit the growth of the other, so churches in a close locality can mean 'competition' and limited growth.

There was a similar, though less extreme story, from a Presbyterian church in Brazil:

- What prevented us from starting the work was a congregation that was already prepared to come. We tried to support them, however, a good part of the group that would make up the congregation came from a split and they were people that were not teachable.

- What caused us to dwindle and close? I believe that it was with the news of another congregation already on the road to start.

There can be a real danger in our lack of collaboration, that gospel effort and resources can be wasted with different groups seeking to do very similar things. An example of where this has been done better than in other places, is in Birmingham, UK. The Birmingham Collective (mentioned in Pitfall 2) is a collaborative church planting network that sought to plant twenty churches by 2020. They succeeded in this, and the hope now is to plant thirty more by 2030.

Andy Weatherley, one of the trustees writes:

The Birmingham Collective (formally 2020 Birmingham) is a collaboration between various churches and mission agencies to see church plants flourishing and multiplying to see the lost come to Christ and the city of Birmingham transformed.

The collective came together out of a missional desperation, church leaders from different denominations praying for one another and various church planting efforts. We exist as a cross denominational body because we recognise that a single church or denomination does not have the resources, skills, abilities or calling to reach the whole city for Christ on its own. We share a conviction that the kingdom of God is designed such that we are stronger and more effective together than we are on our own.

The collective provides training, support, coaching and limited funding for church planters and their spouses through the monthly planters forum, training programmes and retreats. We also facilitate coaching, spouses' meet ups or just a chance to meet with an experienced church planter over coffee. We meet monthly in a planters' forum to provide peer to peer care, prayer and focussed training to develop church leaders and planters. God has used the collective to provide help, inspiration, encouragement and valuable training that has enabled church planters to thrive in areas where they might otherwise have failed.[1]

THE SCRIPTURES

The idea of ministry 'strategy' is something that can easily divide Christians.

As you sweep over the Scriptures, the means by which the Lord accomplishes His purposes and grows His kingdom, are, more often than not, through the unexpected. Whether an aged Abraham who is asked to trust God, leave his home and travel to an unknown destination, or a murdering Moses who speaks with a stutter and would rather the Lord would send someone else. Whether a David who was the smallest of the shepherd-brothers (and, later, a prolific sinner who abused his power), or indeed a bunch of rag-tag fishermen, disciples and tax collectors—the mediocre and marginalised of society. Notwithstanding the King Himself: born not in a palace but an animal shed, largely at home in the villages and the outskirts, with nowhere to lay His head, who wore not a crown of gold but rather a crown of thorns.

Then again, it's not as if God always chooses the person on the lowest rung of the societal ladder in order to do His work. As Paul—who had himself been a promising academic and a rising star within the Jewish religious establishment— writes to the church in Corinth:

> Brothers and sisters, think of what you were when you were called. Not many of you were wise by human standards; not many were influential; not many were of noble birth. But God chose the foolish things of the world to shame the wise; God chose the weak things of the world to shame the strong. God chose the lowly things of this world and the despised things—and the things that are not—to nullify

---

1. https://www.birminghamcollective.org/

the things that are, so that no one may boast before him
(1 Cor. 1:26-29).

By implication, it would seem that some members of the
Corinthian church were wise, influential, and of noble birth.
Scattered through the storyline of the Scriptures, God does
raise up extraordinary individuals, like a Daniel or an Esther,
'for such a time as this' (Esther 4:4), people who were in a
position to intercede for God's people at a time of intense
persecution. Think also of Nehemiah, who, from his place as
the king's cupbearer (Neh. 1:11), was able to plead the case
of his people, and to bring about the return to Jerusalem
and its rebuilding.

The danger, however, is that when we come to forming
the strategy for church planting, churches (or networks) only
think in terms of the latter option—targeting particular cities
that will bring an opportunity to influence a wider region.
Rather than seeking to impact an unreached area with the
gospel of Christ, in and among the primary motivations is a
quiet (or loud …) desire to get our network on a map.

What are we to think about this? Paul's Missionary
Methods: in his time and ours[2] is a collection of essays
seeking to explore where Paul chose to plant and why. Even
within the book a tension exists between some who argue
he chose to settle in diverse centres of higher influence,
that would then plant on hoping to reach further into the
province, and others who argue that he chose the cities
he did because they had both a synagogue and a high
Gentile population, because of some proximity (and hence
support) to other churches, and indeed simply through
pre-existing relationships.

As a church or network considers planting, something
of the tension that exists within the Bible ought to be
prayerfully considered. There is a 'strategic need' to reach

2. Plummer, 2013.

a people with the gospel who are not currently being reached—and there are huge parts of the globe where that is the case—and it is sensible to plan well, and to consider establishing central hubs from which other provinces and peoples can be more easily reached in the longer term. Many are concerned that the next step, the 'trickle-down effect' from the urban centres and outwards, while nice on paper, simply does not happen.

SELF-EXAMINATION

These questions can be used for personal reflection, but also can productively be used within a smaller group. Where you see the word 'you' that can work as both a singular and a plural!

1. What do you make of the desire for networks or denominations to plant churches in 'strategic' centres? What kind of places are seen as strategic and why?

2. What are the strengths and weaknesses of this kind of approach?

3. Is your plant 'strategic'? Why or why not?

4. Who has shaped the vision of your plant? You? A leadership team? The core group? The congregation? The denomination / stream / planting network?

5. What churches are already in the place that you're planning to plant? How would they be affected by your plans?

SUCCESSES AND STRATEGIES

In 2012, the Lord opened the doors for a church plant in Budrio, encouraging us to embrace the vision of church planting in this market town in rural northern Italy. From the beginning, the reaction of city churches in the area has been very positive, especially from the two churches that actively supported the planting of Chiesa la Piazza (Church at the marketplace – Acts 17:17). Yet, mainly due to inexperience on our part and on the part of those churches, almost immediately we began to suffer from the typical rural/urban problem. While the Lord blessed us with conversions of people from our market town, several Christian families who already lived in and around Budrio, continued to prefer the stability and richness of ministries offered by city churches, choosing to travel half an hour or more to reach them. Addressing the issue with the churches that supported us, the theme of casting the vision of rural church planting to these Christians emerged, but often ended in the fact that they were not ready to embrace it! This situation led over time to a sense of frustration on our part, which we had to face, and are facing in the Lord. In these ten years, what the Lord changed was not so much the situation, but our attitude. We decided to continue to invest in the relationship with city churches, participating in joint events, sharing resources, organizing projects together, trying to be a blessing from the countryside to the city.

Then last year we found ourselves in the situation of putting our desires for the gospel and lessons 'learned' into practice. A very gifted couple with three children started attending our fellowship and fell in love with the church's vision of living and reaching out to the community in which we live. In a short time, they settled in, became involved and were loved by our church family. The only problem was that when they met us, they had just purchased a house in the nearby town where there is an Acts 29 church plant. At that point our missional vision of ecclesiology and ministry was tested! We confronted them, seeing two alternatives: either the Lord was calling them to Budrio, then to sell the house they had just bought, or He would give them a heart for Imola and the church plant in that town. Over the months we have accompanied them to get to know the Chiesa la Rocca (The Rock Church), and in a clear way the Lord has guided them to flourish in that church, teaching our church the joy, not always easy to learn, of blessing another church by giving the gifts that are the Lord's.

To this day, our desire is to continue to live out the gospel of the Kingdom in our community and invest ourselves in relationships with city churches, for the glory of the Christ who: 'went throughout all the cities and villages, teaching in their synagogues and proclaiming the gospel of the kingdom and healing every disease and every affliction' (Matt. 9:35).

Stefano & Jennifer Mariotti
Chiesa la Piazza, Italy

Further reading and resources for this chapter

- Timothy Keller, *Center Church: Doing Balanced, Gospel-Centered Ministry in Your City*, (Zondervan, 2015)
- Robert L Plummer and John Mark Terry (Eds) *Paul's Missionary Methods in His Time and Ours* (IVP, 2013)

PITFALL 9

🔥 PARENT CHURCH RELATIONSHIP 🔥

A clear and thriving plant and parent church relationship is one key to church planting health

THE STORY

They were **obviously** massively thankful for the support and partnership from the parent church but things were taking longer than expected, and a number within the core planting team were growing restless and frustrated. The vision was solidifying, the strategy was becoming clearer, the team was increasingly unified, and yet the sending church was unwilling to sign-off on an actual launch date. On top of that, other Christians from the local area who had not even been a part of Trinity church had joined the core team, and they were pushing for the 'cord to be cut' and to get going. Why did they need the support of Trinity anyway? On the other hand, what right did they have to wade in and complicate things?

Before leaving there had been a number of heated leadership-level discussions with the mother church pastor. Difficult questions were raised, and he urged caution, and pleaded with them not to rush into it. As their momentum was building, however, their patience grew thin. And so, somewhat like a petulant teenager who's outgrown the family home, the plant launched out into the big wide world with much optimism and expectation. From the outside, at the outset everything looked healthy and fine.

Hindsight is a beautiful thing but, in the months and years to come the plant leadership came to realise that the pre-launch questions that had been asked were not difficult or awkward, but rather kind questions that came from years of humble pastoral ministry. And indeed, when those anticipated problems came some way down the line, the ties with the mother church had been significantly weakened, and there was a mutual lack of trust and a need to rebuild relationships before either party was prepared to give and receive advice and help.

Looking back, the plant leadership could now see that many within their core team were not really excited by the vision of a new church plant, but more by the vision of leaving the mother church behind. Which, in reality, is not a particularly healthy way to start a new church.

The Study

The point of parenting, certainly in secular terms, is the raising of a well-adjusted, independent young adult, ready to take on the world. There (usually) comes a point when we have to say goodbye. And yet, the independence that young people long for can easily create tension through the teenage years. Life at home can be complicated with clashing rules or cultures or values. This can, and often does, lead to conflict in one form or another. In those moments life in the real world can seem very attractive for a young person. Rather like that of a frustrated teenager who has longed to be rid of the shackles of the family home, the relationship between a plant and a parent church can often become thorny.

Whether it's the desire of the planting team to leave too quickly, or the reluctance of the parent church to snip the cord, or send their 'best' people, or finances, or whether it's a blend of all these things, leaving home can be a minefield. From my experience of both sides of this dynamic, planting is painful for both the parent church and the plant.

Have a listen again to some of the respondents:

- The vision was unclear when I joined the team. A lot of disparaging things were said about 'big church' and 'attractional church' (which pained me, because they were often said at the parent church in ways that seemed to reflect badly on it).

- For churches sending people - support your plants properly. Be generous with people, training and time. Assume it will be harder than they think it will be. Keep praying for them first with urgency then with joy. Give them the chance to share their triumphs, weep and mourn with them when they fail. Establish clear lines of accountability and mentoring. Make sure it's clear who will be providing what support and find the right experience if you don't have it. Support your planters' families.

- Get a supportive church to back you to the hilt and get the nature of that support in writing. Don't let it be vague or assumed.

- One church, which we had been told would support us and send people, was outwardly supportive but in practice discouraged people from coming with us to the extent that no one came. They had the most people living in the area of any of the local churches and had been praying for a plant in the area for a little while, so this was pretty tough to take. One of our parent churches also put some (retrospectively foolish) restrictions on when we were allowed to start talking to people about the plant and inviting them to join, giving us too short a window to recruit people.

- Relationship with the mother church soured very quickly. We did not set clear expectations of the relationship.

There are two clear challenges here. If you are a planter then you must leave well. If you are the parent church then you must send well. This tension needs to be navigated carefully; there are two key ideas that can help us do that well.

1. Clarity

As you can see above, a number of planters longed for clearer and more specific expectations as to what the ongoing relationship with the parent church would look like. Perhaps the understanding that this was necessary only came with hindsight when they experienced the difficulties of planting, and when they realised that they had been naïve, and had imbibed too much of the prevailing success culture that we spoke about in chapter 7.

It's important to be clear on a number of questions:

- **Practically** - exactly how the plant will be supported, and for how long? Is there office space, for example, that the planter can use? How about admin time or supplies, printers or projectors?
- Will it be supported **financially**? How much and for how long? Is this a realistic timescale for this context? How secure is this agreement? What will happen if the mother church's finances are tight?

- **Relationally** – will there be ongoing mentoring? How often, for whom, with whom and for how long? How will the time be earmarked and prioritised?
- Would the parent church consider encouraging and sending more **people** in the fragile early stages, if they are needed? How many and who gets to decide?
- Who gets to decide if the plant is not viable and might need to 'come back'? Who gets to decide when this is? Is the church plant aware of this?

To gain and maintain clarity on questions like these (and more), some mother/daughter churches have adopted Memorandums of Understanding whereby both agree and sign a 'contract' before the plant starts to meet. In Appendix 3 there are a number of questions to ask as you formulate an understanding with respect to ongoing expectations.

2. Charity
For many in the 'church planting world' there's a desire to be 'a church that plants churches', and yet few perhaps realise just how costly the process is. In order to plant well both the mother and daughter church need to show a generosity of spirit towards one another. The mother church ought to allow the daughter church to 'beg, borrow, barter and steal' what it needs to make the launch happen. All too often a plant can be a nice idea on paper, but at the end of the day, in reality certain people might be off limits. The parent ought to be as charitable as possible to enable this new church body to have the best possible opportunity to thrive and flourish. However, it's vital that the plant is also able to show a similar generosity of spirit to the parent church, with an awareness of how much a plant costs the mother church in terms of people, resources, and time. The plant must be generous in its attitude towards the parent church, and intentional about not behaving like that frustrated, petulant teenager.

Planters also need to be aware that some members will decide to join the endeavour, not because of a desire to be part of the vision, but because in all honesty they are frustrated with the parent church and see the plant as the answer to their problems. Maybe they think that the parent church has become too big and the plant will be more intimate? Maybe they think that it's become too set in its ways and the plant will be more innovative? Maybe they think it's too traditional and that the plant will be more informal? Maybe they think it's drifted in terms of vision and the plant will have more of a focus on the things that matter?

Managing those relationships and expectations will be complex. From my experience, it can be far too easy and common to find a disgruntled faction within the plant (at times even on the leadership team), keen to be done with whatever they perceive to be holding them back.

PATIENCE!

Which leads to another necessary fruit of a generous spirit between mother and daughter church – patience! A generous helping of patience is needed all round! Perhaps, because the church planting process can end up being messy with all kinds of unexpected snags and unforeseen challenges, perhaps because of some of the expectations and frustrations already listed in this chapter, but also, sometimes, because there's a desire to move things too quickly and expect independence too soon.

The desire to fly the nest is by no means a bad thing. As with parenting, independence in planting is a key goal. It's new and exciting, they want to get going and live out the vision: to find a place to meet, to reach the new area, become entirely independent, and cut the cord.

When a church plant launches from a parent church, patience is of the utmost importance because, the reality is, there can be a variety of stages towards true independence –

whether legal, financial or, relational and each one will take a level of wisdom and patience. *Im*patience on the part of the plant can all too easily result in difficulties down the line when hurdles are encountered and help is needed in one or more areas. Loosen the ties too quickly and there won't be the relational capital there if they need advice or assistance with hard pastoral situations, or if an unexpected cost has come in, or if members of the core team are in need of old friendships to fall back on when they feel down. Leave too quickly, or don't leave well, and there is a real danger that there won't be any support available when it's needed, and the plant will suffer.

Wise planters listen well and are patient. I'm reminded of the – almost certainly apocryphal – quote from Mark Twain that goes something along the lines of:

> … when I was a boy of fourteen my father was so ignorant, I could hardly stand to have the old man around. But when I got to twenty-one, I was astonished by how much he had learned in seven years.

The need for parents

Forty-nine per cent of the planting stories came from churches that were planted from a parent church (a further 3 per cent were later adopted by a parent church as they realised they needed it), however of the 48 per cent who were without a parent (this number might seem high, but if you dig into the data it's clear that a number were planted from mission agencies in different parts of the world) a group realised they needed greater support and accountability. Asked how they would do it differently if they were to plant again, they said:

- Having a supporting church would be crucial.

- Have a parent church and intentional coaching.

- Find a church to help us, who has the same vision and has experience.

- Have a planting church with accountability at eldership level. Start slowly and make sure of what the vision is and what it would look like in practice.

A word of caution for planters (and their parents)

Having experienced the joy of being both the planter, and the pastor of a church who plants, I am convinced that it is important for the planter to realise the long-term impact on the parent church when a team is sent. In all honesty, I'm not sure I realised that as the planter. When we planted, we were sent with a very strong core team, to the extent that it took somewhere near a decade for the parent church to consider planting again. They lost a generation of leaders. The parent was so exhausted by the process that it took a long time for them to consider having children again. Of course, it made our planting process relatively easy, but, in hindsight, I wonder whether it was unwise in terms of future planting capacity around the city: perhaps they let us take too many of their people and ended up hamstrung?

THE SCRIPTURES

As we consider a healthy mother-daughter church plant relationship, the book of Proverbs brings particular insight as much of it outlines the relationship between a child and their parents. The plant is ideally sent from a pre-existing relationship, with the planter having ministered alongside the sending pastor. This kind of bedrock of relationship yields benefits down the line ...

Humility

Humility, as we discussed in chapters one and two, is a vital starting point for anyone who follows Christ, let alone a church planter. Our posture before the Lord and towards others speaks volumes about our understanding of both our own sin and our grasp of grace. Humility in church planting is not simply the responsibility of individuals, though; indeed, it should be the posture of the whole church plant towards the mother church.

Following the prologue to the book, Solomon immediately urges his child:

> Listen, my son, to your father's instruction
>   and do not forsake your mother's teaching.
> They are a garland to grace your head
>   and a chain to adorn your neck (Prov. 1:8-9).

Rather than humility, plants at times can have a proud posture that struggles to listen or learn, seeks to 'fly the nest' and leave the parent church behind as quickly as possible, longing for independence. Better a humility that is prepared to go at the pace of the other.

Patience

God is infinitely patient and forbearing with us as His children. Set against this, impatience is a hallmark of our culture: the modern world is always rushing and always busy; not only do we struggle to slow down and rest, but we struggle when the queue in a shop is moving too slowly or when the WiFi is glitchy! Perhaps this impatience is even more true of church planters, who are often young, zealous and keen to get going with the project? The Bible never paints rushing in a positive light. Indeed, throughout the Bible we frequently find calls for the people of God to be thoughtful, considered, and prayerful. Wisdom and rushing do not easily go hand in hand. Proverbs highlights the importance of patience for living a life guided by godly wisdom:

> Whoever is patient has great understanding, but one who is quick-tempered displays folly (Prov. 14:29).

> A hot-tempered person stirs up conflict, but the one who is patient calms a quarrel (Prov. 15:18).

> Better a patient person than a warrior, one with self-control than one who takes a city (Prov. 16:32).

Generosity

Both the plant and the parent should work to maintain a posture of kindness and generosity toward one another. The parent needs to be generous toward the plant by, as far as is possible, giving and sending in such a way that the plant can hit the ground running as it launches. The plant, though, needs to reciprocate with generosity of spirit towards the parent, humbly recognising the cost both of sending and of ongoing support.

Proverbs again provides a helpful framework for thinking about this issue:

> A generous person will prosper; whoever refreshes others will be refreshed (Prov. 11:25).

We have a generous God who has taken on flesh and poured Himself out in our place. He provides both the example and the enabling to do likewise. Consideration of this fact along with the verse above will help both sides to refrain from being stingy with resources, time, or attitudes toward one another.

SELF-EXAMINATION

These questions can be used for personal reflection, but also can productively be used within a smaller group. Where you see the word 'you' that can work as both a singular and a plural!

1. What will you miss most about your parent church? What will you not miss?

2. If you're planting from a parent church, have you discussed clear expectations of how they will support you and for how long? What do you think that will look like? Make sure it's written down and check that the parent church agrees! The MOU questions in Appendix 3 might help you broach and structure this.

3. How many people within the core team do you think are coming because they are disappointed with the parent church? How can you help them to leave well? How can you help manage their expectations about where the new plant might not be the answer to their frustrations?

4. Do you have an agreed timeline towards independence? How did you construct it? What are the most likely reasons for overrunning?

SUCCESSES AND STRATEGIES

Without doubt the key factor in our partnership with our sending church (Grace Church) that made our partnership a success was the quality of the relationship and trust we had established at the leadership level.

Andy Weatherley (Pastor at Grace Church) and I had a strong relationship and a shared vision which enabled us to navigate the inevitable challenges and pitfalls of church planting well together. Andy once joked that it was a miracle that we had planted a church together without falling out! We managed that by God's grace because we prioritised the relationship over the project.

For us it was five years of partnership in planting The Gate Church – from early discussions, through to launch, then on to leaving the sending church and finally establishing long term health and viability as an independent church. This was a big commitment for all involved. We worked hard to give time and attention to the key areas of the life of a church plant together throughout this time.

Early on, we came to a shared understanding and conviction of our vision and the philosophy of ministry for the church. This was similar to Grace Church's, but very importantly it was not exactly the same and Andy was very clear and supportive in this being shaped in a way that reflected not only my convictions but also our context.

An area of challenge for us in the early days was the lack of leaders alongside me and so we worked closely together on raising up leaders. Whilst we did that the elders of Grace Church acted as an elder board overseeing The Gate Church along with me and helping with a significant proportion of the preaching and teaching. This involved much time and sacrifice, for example Andy preaching at two services a Sunday most weeks for over two years – often bringing his family with him. It was an invaluable support that meant I was not isolated as a church planter and gave me time, space and support to find my feet in ministry.

Finances and governance were other key areas of partnership. Although Grace Church was only able to send us off with £3,000, they ringfenced the donations from the members in our core team for the church plant and helped us to access grant funding through their networks. During the early years Grace Church also covered certain costs for us, such as insurance and web/email hosting. When it came to constituting as a church we were able to draw on the experience and governing documents of Grace Church.

Although we no longer have any formal connection as churches our relationship remains strong due to the quality of our partnership.'

Jonny Richards
The Gate Church, Birmingham, UK

Further reading and resources for this chapter

- Ed Stetzer, Daniel Im, *Planting Missional Churches: Your Guide to Starting Churches That Multiply* (Broadman and Holman Publishers, 2nd ed., 2016).
- https://www.newchurches.com/podcasts/new-churches-podcast/sending-churches-from-parent-to-partner/

PITFALL 10

🌿 CONTEXT 🌿

Knowing who we are and where we are planting the gospel is vital

THE STORY

Toby was particularly keen on 'not re-inventing the wheel' but was instead incredibly adept at trawling the internet, taking and applying ideas from other places and using them in his own context. He didn't doubt that the church needed creative 'blue-sky' thinkers who could engage outside the box, but he just knew that that was not him! He was more of an implementer, someone who could take models and examples from somewhere else, perhaps tweak them a bit, and then use them here.

Which meant, as he and his family courageously packed up all their stuff into boxes, headed overseas and settled with a church planting mission agency far, far from home, before the plane even landed and their possessions even arrived by freight, he knew what he had to do. How? Because he had done the same thing back home for the previous eight years and it had thrived and flourished. There was a timeline with a clear plan and expectation, he knew how he would fill his first weeks and months. He knew where he wanted to be at twelve months, twenty-four months and beyond. He had it all carefully and intricately mapped out.

How different could it be?

The answer, of course, was very different. What he only realised afterwards was that he had never really understood how the new city, the new country even 'worked'. He didn't understand the culture, how people did things around here (and why). He didn't understand where people gathered, or how they communicated, or their fears or daydreams or desires. He had naïvely assumed that 'people were people' that underneath the surface everyone's the same really, and they just need to hear about Jesus. Toby still believed that this was generally true, however, he now realised that misunderstood and fundamental cultural differences can lead, very, very easily, to people talking past each other. He also realised that his model of church was very Western and urban. He had not thought about what small groups might look like in their new context, or a Sunday gathering, or a sermon, or anything really.

THE STUDY

While it's clear that some planters are genuinely blue-sky-thinkers—able to understand an area well, think outside the box, and plant a church or ministry that is appropriate and fruitful in that context—having spent a lot of time with planters, from my vantage point at least, most are, like Toby in our example above, 'ministry-magpies' – begging, borrowing, and stealing ideas and models from elsewhere, and then implementing them within their own contexts. The key word as we consider this issue is 'assumption'. When our assumptions are incorrect, sooner or later those assumptions will lead to problems.

Planters will often be more aware of the differences inherent within a new context when planting overseas. They are willing, for example, to set aside time to acquire the language and learn about the culture and history. As we'll see, though, even this approach doesn't always work, and we can make wrong assumptions about the different culture(s) within our home country, or even within a single city. Planters can assume they are familiar with an area, but then make incorrect assumptions about who lives here or how this part of town works. Perhaps in our impatience, or naivety, or even a lack of self-awareness, when we simply 'copy and paste' a model from elsewhere we run the risk of problems a little way down the line.

There were a few examples in our study of how the 'copy and paste' strategy led to issues:

1. Leadership problems

Although there can be some overlap, there can be a danger of thinking about church leadership as synonymous with general leadership in the world. We can easily be tempted to raise up church leaders because they lead in their work or business context.

One interesting example of this came from an American cross-cultural church planter, planting in rural Papua New Guinea. Their plan had been to largely engage first with the tribal elders, taking the gospel of Jesus to them. They prayed for fruitfulness, but also that God would raise up from among these elders the first generation of indigenous leadership. Sounds like a good plan. The reason it didn't work was partly a lack of fruit amongst the high echelons of the tribal groupings, but also in large part because Christian leadership – servant leadership – is something very, very different from tribal leadership. They had assumed that brand-new Christians would be able to take the reins, but that wasn't the case. Instead what happened was the church grew quickly among those who had been marginalised in their culture, and there was an ongoing dependency upon the Western missionaries to lead.

2. Financial problems

One common pattern in a number of plants seeking to get established in areas of deprivation was that the parent church, network or denomination had unrealistic expectations about how long it would take for the church to get established and so how long (and how much) external funding would be required.

The issue in this context is that 'we assume that we understand how funding will work, because that was how it worked in our other plant'. More on this issue in chapter eleven.

3. Understanding the area problems

One of the joys of planting is that you can try new things and if they don't work then that's okay. Learning from mistakes represents a great opportunity for further growth and maturation as a church. Here's an example of a plant that attempted a ministry (that they had learnt about from elsewhere), but then after a few months abandoned the idea in favour of something more suitable:

- As a young church plant we wanted to reach out to all the people in our area and so started a number of ministries to attempt to reach out to the different groups. We heard from a church in a different town about an hour away who had a fruitful film night event (it was called Reel-Life!). It was an opportunity to watch a recent film with a projector, eat popcorn and then afterwards around tables discuss the story and ideas being portrayed, hoping to build relationships and help people engage with the themes in a way that would point to Christ. We tried it for a few months and no one really came! Probably because our area was less interested in films, but also that we didn't really have the long-term trust and friendships, that meant people would come and spend an evening with us in our building.

One planter commented that we desperately need more models to reach the breadth of our increasingly diverse and complicated world.

- We are desperately in need of NEW ways of thinking about church planting, we need many forms. This is risky and we need to be willing to take those risks.

THE SCRIPTURES
Paul's contextualisation

Our Triune God, by His very nature, is willing to act and communicate in a way that is appropriate to reach a people for Himself. As His Son takes on flesh, ultimately to die and be raised again in our place, so at the very heart of who God is, we see a God who condescends Himself in love for others. He lovingly serves to achieve His 'purposes'. As we follow a king who is ready to appropriately 'flex' His methodology, so we see Paul's example and desire to use his freedom for the good of others, that he might reach as many as possible with the gospel of Christ. He did not simply 'copy and paste'. Have a listen as he wrote to the church in Corinth.

> Though I am free and belong to no one, I have made myself a slave to everyone, to win as many as possible. To the Jews I became like a Jew, to win the Jews. To those under the law I became like one under the law (though I myself am not under the law), so as to win those under the law. To those not having the law I became like one not having the law (though I am not free from God's law but am under Christ's law), so as to win those not having the law. To the weak I became weak, to win the weak. I have become all things to all people so that by all possible means I might save some. I do all this for the sake of the gospel, that I may share in its blessings (1 Cor. 9:19-23).

Like a rock dropping into the middle of a lake, the Spirit is poured out equipping His people, and the gospel ripples travel to 'Jerusalem, Judea, Samaria and the end of the earth' (Acts 1:8). As the early church spread, Paul and Peter's methods varied depending on the city and context that they arrived in. There is no 'one-size-fits-all'. Paul will usually seek out the synagogue before heading to the gentiles, but then he will endeavour to understand the nature of the city he's arrived in, before appropriately sharing the message of Christ in that city.

Preaching in Acts

Much has been written regarding the diverse messages within the book of Acts as Paul takes the message of the gospel to different cities. The juxtaposition of methodology between a 'synagogue-sermon' in Pisidian Antioch (Acts 13:16-41) against a gentile audience in Lystra and Derbe (Acts 14:14-17) is striking. Whilst there are obvious similarities—at the heart of both sermons there is an all-powerful God (13:16-22 and 14:17) and a criticism of both congregations for seeking salvation through the wrong means (13:39 and 14:15)—the differences are noteworthy.

Paul bases his arguments on an appropriate authority for each context. In Pisidian Antioch he focuses his message on the Old Testament text and the message of John the Baptist; in Lystra his emphasis is on general revelation. In Chapter 13, Paul turns his focus to their need for Christ, while in Chapter 14 he urges his congregation to turn away from idols that cannot bring joy toward the living God.

If Paul takes an appropriate message to different contexts and audiences, is the same true for how he sought to establish new churches? From what we can tell, it looks like it.

Planting in diverse Antioch

One great example of contextualised church planting is the establishment of a fruitful church in the diverse metropolis of

Antioch. The gospel arrives via persecution but quickly takes root with a strikingly diverse leadership team (Acts 13:1): a global leadership for a global city. Some of the leaders would have been classically educated, speaking a diversity of languages; some would have been brought up with extreme wealth and opportunity; some would have arrived with little, probably from Jewish backgrounds, escaping persecution. This was a leadership drawn from diverse ethnicities, economic strata, and educational groupings, yet united in seeking to establish a church in this sprawling metropolis. In the time that Luke wrote historians speak of at least eighteen different isolated ethnic groups within the city, largely divided from one another.

Self-examination

These questions can be used for personal reflection, but also can productively be used within a smaller group. Where you see the word 'you' that can work as both a singular and a plural!

1. How well do you think you understand the area into which you are planting?

2. How can you get to know your area better? Have you done any work with the census data? Who lives here? Think educationally, economically, ethnically, politically. How might that shape your plans to reach them with the gospel? What do people live for here? What are their fears and struggles? Where do they gather?

3. What planting models / examples have most shaped your planting methodology? Where do you have doubts that they will work in the way you want?

4. Are there any key assumptions that you have made in your plan that you ought to revisit?

SUCCESSES AND STRATEGIES

The Lord Jesus is pretty clear on what He wanted His disciples to do if somebody has sinned against them. He explains in Matthew 18:15: 'If your brother sins against you, go and tell him his fault, between you and him alone. If he listens to you, you have gained your brother' (ESV).

However, in a Japanese context, this would be considered way too direct a method of communication. Indeed, direct communication might cause someone to be offended, and perhaps cause them to feel some sense of shame, and upset the relational harmony, which is valued so highly. It would be considered rude. Therefore, almost nobody would communicate as directly as this. Rather, if someone feels that you have wronged them in some way, they would speak to somebody who is close to you. That person would then have the responsibility to convey the message to you. Then, you might consider your response, and pass the message back via the intermediary to the person who felt aggrieved.

I was recently made aware of a great example of this. A friend was asked to make a simple Japanese rice dish for a social gathering after church one Sunday lunchtime. But, having found that the resulting dish was not as it perhaps traditionally tastes, one of the church leaders tried to take action. However, instead of speaking to my friend about it, the church leader instead spoke to my friend's wife about it a few days later. The wife then was the intermediary, who relayed the information to my friend.

Whether regarding a mere difference of opinion or a sin, conflict avoidance is the pattern. Do we stick to the cultural way of avoiding any potential conflict, or do we follow Jesus' teaching of speaking to someone directly, just the two of you? I think that this is an example of how we need to be sensitive and see the positive features of the cultural norm, but also stick to Jesus' teaching, despite the Japanese culture.

Thierry Richards
Pastor, Marunouchi Church Tokyo
Senior Partner, Tokyo Marunouchi Partnership

Further reading and resources for this chapter

- Timothy Keller, *Center Church: Doing Balanced, Gospel-Centered Ministry in Your City,* (Zondervan, 2015)
- Craig Ott and Gene Wilson, *Global Church Planting* (Baker Academic, 2011)
- Stefan Paas, *Church Planting in The Secular West* (Wm.B.Eerdmans Publishing Co, 2016)

PITFALL 11

❧ PRACTICAL ISSUES ❧

Unforeseen challenges, finances, staffing needs are all major hurdles in the work of planting

THE STORY

From even before the launch day it had been a struggle. Coming from a large and 'polished' congregation of 850, they had prayed for 100 people but had only ended up with thirty-eight, prayed for a decent core leadership team of twelve but it had been five. Fundraising was a similar story, and the practicalities of acquiring equipment hadn't gone too well either. Eventually they found an old school hall to meet in, but it wasn't quite in the area they had prayed and planned for, and it had no real parking. The planter often spoke of the leadership team as being like the proverbial swan gracefully swimming across the water, but underneath a crazy amount of energy, effort, and hustle, trying to keep things afloat. They hadn't even officially launched, but everything felt like a battle (and everyone was feeling more and more frustrated and burnt out).

Encouragingly, the launch service was overflowing, but it was mostly full of well-wishers from the parent church as well as friends and supporters from down the years. By the next week numbers had dropped a bit, but then by the week after it was down to forty. They had picked up a couple of local Christians who were keen to 'try them out for a season' but that was about it. Week by week, Sundays came together and they made do and got by, but the sheer number and level of expectations became draining: the level of preparation for the kids groups, the sound of the full-band, the exceptional tech, and the design output ... Their parent church was so polished and 'together', and they wanted the plant to be the same.

Those involved in the financial decisions knew that the money was drying up. They had budgeted assuming rapid growth, but in the planter's mind it felt like, in all honesty, the Lord had it in for them. Was He really the 'Loving Father who owns the cattle on a thousand hills and knows what we need'? Or actually a stingy dad who's not up for passing on what His kids want?

Months on, when gently pressed by fellow planters within his 'planting cohort' as to whether this vision was actually what God wanted, or what he wanted, the planter was left speechless. And when challenged to write down what was actually needed to start a new church, he found that he couldn't. Maybe he needed to go back to the drawing board and rethink? But before that maybe he needed to pray?

The Study

As you can imagine, within a study of eighty churches from diverse settings and contexts around the globe, there were a variety of practical issues that respondents mentioned, either things that they did not have they would have liked, or else unforeseen problems and challenges.

First of all, we'll consider some of the unmet needs (or wants) before thinking about unforeseen problems.

1. Unmet needs

Sometimes, in His providence, the Lord doesn't provide in the way that we want Him to. Listen to this lengthy example from a medium-sized plant in the South-Eastern United States that highlights the three most common unmet needs:

- After eight years we still do not have a building and within our context this makes us seem like we are not legit. We are meeting inside of another church on Sunday mornings at 8:00 am while we raise money. For the first seven-and-a-half years we were a mobile church.

- We still don't have a quality worship leader/band. We simply cannot get anyone to come and serve in this capacity. I was playing guitar/singing/and preaching for several years. Currently we have a member who leads us in worship through tracks because it is the best we can do.

- We often hear we don't provide enough for kids or youth group. Several have left over the years because of this. If you are a non-Christian who is actually looking for a church home it would be much easier and more attractive to simply drive a few more miles down the road and have a 'buffet' of times, ministries, etc for you and your family. It can often be difficult to see all that we do have at Mission because of all that we don't have.

Of those who struggled and felt unsupported by either their parent church or network, 36 per cent said that they would have liked more help from more people, another 36 per cent simply spoke of their desire for emotional support, whilst 18 per cent mentioned finances as a significantly limiting factor.

- We launched with a small core team, and I wouldn't ever do that again. I would want a core team of at least fifty adults. This would give you the manpower, the money, and the momentum needed in church planting.

- Lack of resources for handling small children during meetings.

- Challenging to have consistent kids work – struggled with volunteers initially.

- Adequate finances, more human resources and practical partnership.

- More supporters, more people helping with money, because we need money to pay all bills.

- Bigger core team, raise enough money to hire part-time worship staff to start.

- The finances from the main church and the sister churches pulled out of the support and this brought a lot of challenges in our ministry.

As we saw in the previous chapter, the lack of consideration for socio-economic context in most funding grants is a common complaint. It seems that many of our financial planting models are based upon projects in upwardly mobile urban areas where growth and self-sustainability is quicker, rather than in more deprived areas with a lower average income. One example from Canada:

- I think a three-year diminishing subsidy in today's cultural context is unrealistic for planters. It should be extended to five years for our type of plant.

As well as naïve expectations of financial sufficiency, one respondent pointed the finger at their church planting network, which, they perceive, is selective in its support and distribution of funds:

- One thing I would say is that there is no financial support offered from the network for churches that are small. It seems they want to get behind winning teams, as it were. I think some of this philosophy is wrong-headed and some plants/planters just need more support at the jump based upon how they started and what the circumstances were.

In addition to these unmet needs, a number of unforeseen problems were listed.

2. Unforeseen challenges
Illnesses, both for the planter and for close family and church members, were an issue, at times creating a significant personal drain for the planter, or indeed leaving them short-staffed and under-resourced as others have to step away from the project:

- I got chronic respiratory and sinus sickness (pneumonia, deep constant cough, bronchitis) which lasted for eight years. It turned out to be from relational and work stress but I didn't know what it was, till the plant ended.

- I have a son with very severe special needs which has caused me to be more limited in time and attention than the typical pastor. Though most of the church is very understanding … personally I feel his illness has limited me in my ability to pastor to my full potential and what the church needs. By 2019 his genetic disorder has gotten worse, and this has forced me to miss several Sundays, and left me generally struggling to preach and lead the way I desire.

- My dad got cancer, so I pulled out emotionally.

- My wife's health and mental breakdown were huge issues.

- The first couple we met were the catalyst for moving us forward to plant. The husband became our first elder, but he was dying. They had to move out of state for his health (he lived!), but they have to stay near their hospital. From that moment onward, I've struggled to get my legs back under me.

Living through the COVID-19 pandemic (data collection was mainly through 2020) has also reminded church planters and pastors everywhere that national and international events can bring with them significant and unforeseen challenges:

- … Not to mention the Covid-19 problem, which stopped a lot of things.

- COVID19. It's hard enough to do pioneering ministry let alone pioneering a church plant in a pandemic.

- Social distancing, government restrictions, physical building limitations …

THE SCRIPTURES
Practical
Provision is tricky. On the one hand, we have a Father in Heaven who owns the cattle on a thousand hills (Ps. 50:10) and knows what we need (Matt. 6:25-34); on the other, we have His perfect will and perfect timing, and His tendency to not quite give us everything we think we need at just the time we think we need it.

God is not stingy or mean. His plans and purposes for us and those around us are more involved than we could ever guess, and He intends that we would learn to trust him: to be dependent upon Him, like the children that we are; to look to Him each and every day for provision, as His people had to in the wilderness of the exodus. When asked how to pray, Jesus teaches His disciples to say: 'give us today our daily bread'. This is expressive of what we need, a daily dependence, a daily trust, a daily relationship with the One who made us.

A big problem for the Western church (particularly) is that we often get muddled up about what we need and what we want. Our prayer ought to be, with wise Agur, in Proverbs 30:8-9:

> Give me neither poverty nor riches, but give me only my daily bread. Otherwise, I may have too much and disown you and say, 'Who is the Lord?' Or I may become poor and steal, and so dishonour the name of my God.

Our model for church planting can reflect this messy muddle, as at times we might desire the big and bold, trusting in those things to cause a splash as we plant. Just because God is blessing a planting project, it doesn't necessarily mean He's going to give us everything we long for. Perhaps He's wanting us to continue to look to Him each day for provision, whether that be financial or practical, such as a place to meet, extra people to serve, or equipment that we feel we need.

The main financial model for church planting that I've encountered in the West looks something like this: an individual looking to plant a church from a mother church (or sharing the load among a group of churches) will receive funds from that parent church alongside supplementary income they might raise from other individuals or trust funds to enable launch. The biblical basis often given for this will draw upon the model of the apostle Paul who, for example, gratefully received support from the Philippian church (Phil. 4:10-20), and asked the Roman Church (whom he had never even met in person) to fund him for his desired journey to Spain (Rom. 15:20-24). Paul actively seeks to raise funds to take the gospel into a new area, in the hope that it might take root and that churches might then be planted.

It's also true that Paul was a tent maker. He happily engaged in this type of work, unusual for a religious scholar, because he did not want to be a burden to unbelievers or new Christians in a new area, and so he utilised his skills in order to raise funds for a time. It's quite possible that in all four of Paul's missionary journeys he was largely self-funded (see 1 Cor. 9:6, 2 Cor. 11:12, Acts 18:1-5 and Acts 20:33-35). His example in Corinth is particularly instructive for us (see Acts 18:1-5), as it contains several possible parallels to a church planting endeavour. His time in the city is initially self-funded through tent-making, but later, when Silas and Timothy arrive from Macedonia possibly with a gift to help fund him, he then prioritises and focuses solely on preaching and teaching. As well as providing financial support, tent-making created opportunities for conversations (see Acts 18 again) and showed Paul to be a model of hard work and transparency. By working to support himself, Paul demonstrated to the surrounding community that he was not in ministry for selfish gain (like many other travelling orators of the time), but rather paid his own way in a fresh, new territory. Rather than tent-making being a support model that Paul fell back on, what seems more likely is that this was his usual pattern of ministry, despite the fact that he could have asked for support.

The bi-vocational model in church planting is certainly an option that many consider, though from my experience not one that many consider for long. Church planting, especially at the beginning, is labour intensive, and the bi-vocational model is personally costly, but I wonder whether, perhaps especially in secular cities where it is expensive to live, it needs to be an option that is taken increasingly seriously, both as a means to raise funds in the early days (and beyond), but also as a platform for engagement with individuals and the community into which the church is being planted. Paul is mocked for being a tent-maker in 2 Corinthians, the implication being that his ministry is second-rate. Perhaps that view of bi-vocational ministry as being second-best is evident in some church planting circles today? Through social media and mainstream news reporting, the world is very aware of mega-churches and celebrity pastors. Perhaps Paul's witness as one who worked bi-vocationally is one we should take seriously ...

Lastly, I would like to suggest that there's a similar pattern when it comes to other things that we feel we need when we plant. Our dream and vision for our plant, may simply be that: our dream and vision, our desires. Why do we think that we need to plant in that way, with that number of people, and with those ministries up and running from the start? Have we genuinely sought the Lord in this (and we may well have), or simply asked Him to bless our plans? It may be that if He's not providing what we think we need it is because He is teaching us what it means to trust Him, so that we know (a) that we are dependent upon Him and (b) that when He does provide, it is all of Him: we're helpless and so it's obvious that He gets the glory. It may also be that we are asking God for the wrong thing. Perhaps the model we have gone with is overly ambitious or contextually inappropriate, perhaps we need to rethink our strategy or plans? Could it be that we meet in a home for a while? Could it be that some staff need to consider the bi-vocational model? Could it be that we need to rethink ministry structure and have to build it around who we have, rather than what we would like to do?

SELF-EXAMINATION

These questions can be used for personal reflection, but also can productively be used within a smaller group. Where you see the word 'you' that can work as both a singular and a plural!

1. What things do you 'want' for the church plant (desirable) and what things do you think you 'need' (essential)? Why have you made these decisions and distinctions between the wants and the needs?

2. How resilient do you think you are as a planter? How many knock backs can you cope with?

3. Are there any practical things without which you believe the plant cannot function? If (for example) you don't find a suitable building to meet in, how might your vision alter?

4. (If you're not) would you be prepared to be a bi-vocational church planter? If not, why not?

5. What do you think the Lord is teaching us when we don't receive everything we want? What are you tempted to do / feel at that time?

SUCCESSES AND STRATEGIES

There were simply not enough of us. A couple of years after Christ had planted Broadgrace Church in rural Norfolk we saw lots of opportunities for ministry and few brothers or sisters to take them up. We had hardly grown from the core team of around eighteen of us. It was tiring enough simply keeping Sunday meetings, midweek bible studies and other essential parts of church life running.

Then one of the church members suggested that we should pray for five more households to join us over the next year. We were not sure if it was right to ask our Father for a specific number, but decided that He could always choose to send more or less if it was not a right thing to ask. In three years we had seen one or two join us, and as many leave. It seemed to me a ridiculously ambitious prayer but we committed to pray together for the year.

I did not assume the Lord would answer the prayer. But if He did I knew who we needed. We needed wise, godly, mature Christians to move to the area with a heart to roll up their sleeves and get stuck in. We needed brand-new, keen-as-mustard converts who would encourage and inspire us all with the saving power of Christ's gospel.

The Lord sent the five households in an amazing answer to our prayers. Some of them were wise and godly saints. The first couple were not. They were needy, with hurts, illnesses, learning difficulties and all manner of weakness. I was dismayed – we needed helpers and the Lord had sent us people who needed help.

But we did not need helpers. We needed to be a family and I needed to see that church is a family. I had made the subconscious, silly and deeply wicked assumption that some people are capable and serve, others are struggling and need serving. The truth Jesus was teaching me, I think, is that we are all struggling, needy and broken and He serves us. That is how He builds His church. We all need each other. Broadgrace now is a family full of kindness, love and warmth that I find delightful. This Christlike glory was shaped significantly by those who joined us then. When Jesus chooses the weak and foolish things of the world, He knows what He is doing and the gates of hell will not prevail.'

John Hindley
Broadgrace Church, Norfolk, UK

Further reading and resources for this chapter
- Paul Tripp, *Dangerous Calling* (IVP, 2012)
- Colin Marshall and Tony Payne, *The Trellis and the Vine* (Matthias Media, 2021)

PITFALL 12

❧ OPPOSITION ❧

The daily Christian life is a battle and will be until Jesus returns. Church planting is no exception

THE STORY

Christoph, his wife, and their young family had lived in their sleepy little village for most of their married life. Commuting to church on Sunday was fairly standard practice. There was a traditional parish church in their village, but it had no children's ministry and, in all honesty, not very much life or gospel teaching. The church in the neighbouring town, which had all of these things and more, was a much more attractive option. Following the completion of a new housing development, a number of the town church families had begun moving into their village, and the leadership team had begun to consider whether a plant would be strategically wise. A new church to reach all these new locals: a place to invite friends from the village along to.

They leafleted the area, letting the locals know their plans and asking how they thought a new village church might be able to help and serve in this area. On the back of a leaflet was an invite to a community BBQ where people could come and learn more, as well as enjoying a slap-up meal. People came for the food (including a number of key local stakeholders and the village church minister) and were initially polite, but things quickly turned sour when conversation moved onto plans for the plant.

In hindsight, that initial gathering set the tone for the relationship between the new plant and the village community for the years to come. There was always low-level opposition. Locals didn't want 'your sort of church' meeting in their village hall on a Sunday morning: more cars clogging up their roads, the sound of singing waking people up at 10:30, and anyway, what exactly did they believe? The village minister was as, if not more, antagonistic. What was wrong with his church? An influx of young people would be brilliant, they said, bringing in some life and energy – as long as they didn't actually want to change anything, they would be very welcome indeed.

The long-term hostility was exhausting. The day-by-day, week-by-week attempt to block or belittle anything the plant leadership team tried to do. The relational side-lining. The friendships that fell by the wayside. The rolled eyes as they walked into the local supermarket. The collective weight of these things meant that the plant never really gained any traction, that it never thrived, that it just about kept going.

The Study

Church ministry is hard for all kinds of reasons, and the presence of opposition 'in theory' ought not be a surprise to the church planter. In reality, however, opposition often catches us by surprise, usually because it comes from places, and in ways, that are unexpected:

1. Satan

The first source mentioned in the study is spiritual opposition. Pastors can sometimes be slow or cautious to attribute opposition to 'spiritual attack', however a number recognised the daily reality of opposition from Satan seen in a variety of ways.

For example:

- … Satan is serious about coming against you when the kingdom is advancing, prayer has to be at the centre of building church.

- Planting is hard! It needs to be led by the Holy Spirit and I can't control things. There will always be distractions. Satan doesn't want it to grow. The battle isn't fought in the flesh.

2. The world

The second broad area of opposition mentioned was 'the world', those outside the church who are not pleased to find a new church in their neck of the woods. One planter in rural Papua New Guinea spoke of the cost of becoming a believer for those who turned to Christ.

- The believers had extreme external pressures and threats from a traditional cult. Persecution was regular. Most were ostracised from their families. Some could not take this.

Another planter in India stated that:

- Being centrally ruled by religiously majoritarian governments [can] cause lots of obstacles for ministry and church planting.

For those in the increasingly secular West the opposition is (currently) not to the extent faced by many brothers and sisters around the world. We may not face 'sticks and stones' but words can still be very damaging. They can hurt, but more than that, they can cause us to lose confidence in our witness, to slightly 'soften' our message, or 'turn down the volume' a little. The neighbourhood into which you're planting may not welcome you with open arms when they hear that you potentially disagree with them on whatever hot topic twitter is shouting about at the time.

Many planters encountered similar obstacles to those found in India (above). A number reported that finding a venue was particularly difficult, and that an increasing fear of community backlash or being cancelled led venues (even those who needed the money) to refuse to allow churches to rent their space. I've heard stories of local evangelical churches writing to literally hundreds of options and being turned down by all of them because of their orthodox doctrinal convictions.

3. The church

Whilst opposition from outside the church can be painful, opposition from 'within' can be all the more agonising. By this I'm not so much talking about the local church family that's been planted, but rather other local churches, groupings or denominations. Strikingly, this was the main avenue of opposition listed within the study, perhaps because for many it was the most unexpected.

At ground level there will be a spectrum of 'welcome' from the other local churches in your neighbourhood. Some, with varying theological convictions, will not be at all pleased that you are planting into their patch. Your plans or presence might be taken as a criticism or a threat. The idea of you preaching your convictions in their community might even be abhorrent, particularly for those planting within mixed denominations. One local story from my own town saw a number of angry church leaders disgusted to hear of an evangelical church planting (with permission) on their side of town.

Other planters spoke of a welcome, but with some caution when it came down to the question of people.

- ... most local churches were delighted to support us, but were not so happy to give us workers. The church where I was Assistant Pastor actively told me that I couldn't ask people to join us ...

- I think a large city centre [denominational] church choosing to plant on our doorstep has negatively affected our momentum more recently!

As we discussed in chapter eight, hard questions need to be asked regarding geographical priority when it comes to church planting. Planting into 'strategic' centres, at the expense of other churches already labouring there, raises a number of questions regarding wise use of resources and people. The healthy planter will have proactive conversations with local allies in advance. One church planter from an independent church in the UK told the story of a conversation with an anxious neighbouring pastor who said:

- It feels a bit like I'm a small, struggling local supermarket and I've got a large Tesco moving in next door.

From that honest statement, they were able to set some 'parish-boundaries' and agreements as to how they might work together on that side of town, not as competitors but teammates. It set the tone for an ongoing healthy partnership.

As well as 'opposition' (to varying degrees) from local churches, some planters spoke of a very difficult relationship with their network or denomination. The context where this was most painfully evident was within a mixed denomination. This will not only be financially or emotionally costly, but also relationally, as other churches unite against them.

> • Over the time, there was much political (spiritual) opposition from the other [denominational] churches. At times, I would spend a couple of days a week on 'politics' ...

The planter also speaks of 'visceral revulsion' from a neighbouring minister, so much so that confidence was squashed and

> • We had got to a stage where the first question we would ask, when discussing a new idea, was 'are we allowed?'. For all our confidence in God, we were feeling crushed. [...] The reality of 'visceral revulsion' as described earlier meant we did try to be careful.

THE SCRIPTURES

Opposition to the gospel is to be expected. The Bible does not water-down the fact of that: just as people persecuted Christ and the prophets before Him, so those who come after ought also to be aware of, and ready for, that reality. Foundationally, our opposition is not of this world: 'For our struggle is not against flesh and blood, but against the rulers, against the authorities, against the powers of this dark world and against the spiritual forces of evil in the heavenly realms' (Eph. 6:12). Satan does not want new churches established. Satan does not want beacons of light planted in the midst of the darkness. Built upon that foundation though, the faces of opposition for a church will take many forms.

To begin to engage with this truth we will take a look at Paul's relationship both as he plants and supports the young church in Philippi.

In Acts 16 Paul arrives in the city and, following the release of a demon-possessed girl who foretold the future, Paul and his team are imprisoned. They are subsequently freed and, having established a small church, they move on. But the opposition they encountered (mirrored in numerous other towns on Paul's missionary journeys) set the tone for the young Christians they left behind. Opposition will come as people feel threatened by the gospel—in the case of the slave girl's owners it was for financial reasons, for many in our day it will be social or moral. Christians in the West are increasingly being marginalised, and many view the gospel as being 'dangerous'. Clearly, the pressure of local opposition got to the Philippian church because by the time that Paul wrote to them he felt the need to remind them to follow his example in the opposition they are facing (Phil. 1:27-28).

There are at least two other groups of believers or pseudo believers we encounter in the letter as Paul writes to them under house arrest in Rome, the first are a curious group who have seemingly been emboldened to speak the gospel more openly and earnestly, as they see Paul imprisoned (Phil. 1:15-18). His chains give them an impetus to turn up the volume. Perhaps they are a 'rival' gathering of Christians who have taken umbrage with Paul, feeling threatened by him? Perhaps a faction within the early church with a disagreement over secondary matters? Paul is clear that (1) they do it out of selfish ambition but also (2) they are preaching Christ and so, even though they preach from false motives, the message about Christ is getting out and that is the main thing. Our context will no doubt be different, but planters may well encounter other local gospel churches with whom there is an unhealthy competition. We would do well to settle with Paul at this point, happy that they preach the gospel and to view them as brothers and sisters in Christ, even if our relationship with them needs some work.

The second group within the letter are those who consider themselves as belonging to God, but in fact do not. Chapter 3:1-11 spells out their confidence is not in the gospel of Christ, but rather in their bloodlines and their observance of the OT law. Paul is very bold in his condemnation of them. Again a number of planters spoke of opposition from religious, even Christian groups or networks who were opposed to the gospel of Christ and so opposed to churches planting in their town. We would do well to pray that God would open their eyes to their need for a saviour and that forgiveness and favour with God cannot be won through legalistic observance but rather humbly turning to Him in repentance and faith.

SELF-EXAMINATION

These questions can be used for personal reflection, but also can productively be used within a smaller group. Where you see the word 'you' that can work as both a singular and a plural!

1. Where does conflict and opposition come from in ministry? What might it look or sound like in your context?

2. How do you personally cope with conflict and opposition? What areas of conflict are especially difficult for you to deal with? Why?

3. What opposition have you faced in ministry, both from within and outside the church? Have you faced any (so far) if your plant has started?

4. How will you personally cope with this and how will you lead your church through this?

5. Opposition from other local churches can be especially hard to deal with. How proactive have you been in reaching out to them? How can you, as far as possible, model gospel unity?

SUCCESSES AND STRATEGIES

'I thought it would have worked as I planned it.'

Before moving back to Panama as a pastor planter I was advised to plan a well-structured project containing all the things that we (as a family) should really consider regarding our future ministry. Among them we thought about: a good landscape (city and country background), evangelism methodology, an estimated family budget, positive and negative risk management and others.

All of those points mentioned above have a certain predictability, for example: family budget. In our case our support comes mainly from Brazil, so a devaluation of that currency would affect us directly, and would lead us to re-evaluate our budget and seek solutions for this hardship. However, I discovered that that mark of predictability is not really strong in one particular point: the landscape issue. No matter how good our ethnographic, economic and social study of the missionary field is (even for a local, like me, absent for more than seven years), we shouldn't take for granted the certainty of the knowledge of that particular culture as a way to success. It would be better to humble ourselves and accept that, instead of having a 'precise' field view let us work with a 'caricature' field view. I think it is extremely important to recognize this for two reasons: a supposed 'accurate' vision could lead some to a dogmatic rigidity (arrogance), and second, to tragic frustration in the planter (idealized expectations).

In my case I had to deal with that problem. I thought I had a perfect view of my own people and that all the strategies I developed based on that 'accurate knowledge' would definitely work. After some months I realized that the real problem wasn't my strategies but my arrogance and idealized expectation (the root of the problem). I had to understand that a culture is constantly changing, and people are moved and shaped by the cultural spirit of that time and that moment.

To make that clearer, let me give a good example so we can illustrate it and learn from it.

I think of Paul, how he was wise to deal with that, when he humbly approached the people in Athens. It says: 'he was greatly distressed to see that the city was full of idols' (Acts 17.16). He already knew (caricature) that Athenians were pagans, but it was not until he saw (sensitivity) that he distressed himself and then 'reasoned (adaptability) in the synagogue with both Jews and God-fearing Greeks, as well as in the marketplace day by day with those who happened to be there'. We see the same in his preaching at the Areopagus when he said: 'I see that in every way you are very religious. For as I walked around and looked carefully…'.

We should learn from Paul, a master planter, who teaches us to be humble, sensitive and adaptable, never arrogant or idolatrous of his ministry. In prayer and faith, let us be like Paul who 'walked around and looked carefully' so we can 'finish the race and complete the task the Lord Jesus has given us – the task of testifying to the good news of God's grace'. God bless us.

Heber Samuel Rios Caballero
Church planting in Chitré, Panama

Further reading and resources for this chapter
- Tom Bennardo, *The Honest Guide to Church Planting* (Z Carr, 2019)
- https://www.thegospelcoalition.org/article/why-church-planting-so-hard/

❦ CONCLUSION ❦

'Insanity is doing the same thing over and over and expecting different results.'
– Probably not Albert Einstein
(though often attributed to him)

This book has been an attempt to make us stop and listen to the voices of those strugglers from the breadth of 'the church planting world' who have gone before us, to learn from them and so help us not make their mistakes. When voices are unheard or ignored we face the real possibility of simply repeating history again and again and again. And again. And that, as (probably not) Einstein famously said, is insanity.

It's an attempt to forewarn and so forearm us. To make us aware of some of the probable dangers that lurk ahead, whether those from within (us or the church family) or indeed those that lurk outside. When you know what's coming down the road, or at least what is likely to come down the road, you might be better at dealing with it when it arrives.

And so go! Go and plant! Go and partner and sow the beautiful gospel into places where Jesus is not known. Tell those who need to hear. In weakness and humility go and plant healthy, thriving, counter-cultural communities of light that speak of Him and look like Him, into areas of decay and darkness. But as you go, be aware of the challenges that lie on the path ahead ...

And a final word on caring for the injured

I was warned at the outset that speaking to leaders of plants who were not simply 'limping' but had closed down might be a step too far for many. They wouldn't want to talk. They wouldn't want to open up the wounds again. Too much of them had been 'lost' as the project had 'failed' and for many, lives would have taken a significant turn into other industries, or a return to previous paths from before the plant.

I suspect that was true for some. Indeed there were a number of individuals whom I was introduced to and gently pursued to hear their story, but who were unresponsive, unready or unwilling to talk.

There were others though who were only too pleased to have their voice listened to. For them it had felt like they (and the plants they led) had been swept under the carpet, at worst an awkward embarrassment, at best, a statistical anomaly to be explained away as an outlier.

For those who were happy to talk, there was a breadth of health: a number had processed their difficult experiences with a level of objectivity and maturity and had emerged with a better sense of who they were – both in terms of their identity in Christ, but also their character and competencies. Many were still in ministry, but with a better sense of self-awareness and wisdom and so were serving in contexts that better suited them.

It's also fair to say that a number had struggled to process their experiences well. It was clear what they needed was ongoing help to work through what had happened and consider why things hadn't gone as they had hoped. Feelings were complicated and confused. Some were clearly still weary and wounded. Some were grieving. It was surprising to me that so many had received such little help.

I guess this is a call to network leaders, planting coordinators or parent-church pastors (or even adjacent pastors who can see there may be a need) to reach out and care for those who's plants have closed. What would an 'exit interview' look like? What would ongoing care look like? How might you partner with them and help them, not just to finish well, but to consider lessons they have learnt that may be beneficial for others?

Ours is a God who cares for and loves to bind up the broken-hearted (Isa. 61:1), how might we join Him in that task for these bruised and broken friends who have struggled in the field?

APPENDIX 1

The Original Survey

Church planting is hard

Sadly things don't always go as we hoped, planned or prayed they might. In those situations it's good for us to carefully reflect and learn for the future. We hope this piece of research will be useful for different types of people: those who have planted and the plant not worked; for those in the midst of a plant but significantly struggling, and those thinking about planting and wanting to learn the lessons of the past.

To that end we're looking to contact planters from a breadth of planting networks and backgrounds who, for a variety of reasons, haven't ended up planting the churches that they hoped they would – either in church plants that have not lasted or those not currently thriving.

If that's you or you know someone who might fall into that category please pass on as appropriate and, as honestly as you can, fill out the questions below.

We promise that what you say will be treated in strict confidence and with anonymity, unless you are happy to share your experiences – the final few questions will touch on what that might mean.

SECTION 1

1.0 Personal details

1.1 Age categories (Under 25, under 35, 36 and above)

1.2 Married (and if so, for how long)

1.3 Kids (number and ages)

1.4 Previous ministry experience (with details and length)

1.5 Theological training (with details and length)

1.6 How would you describe your theological stream? (For example, Baptistic, Reformed, Contemporary, Traditional etc).

SECTION 2

2.0 Planting details

2.1 Name and location of church plant

2.2 Name and location of 'parent' church (if applicable).

2.3 Distance of plant from 'parent' church (if applicable).

2.4 Describe the area into which you planted (for example was it urban/rural/suburban, social cultural/ethnic demographics, were there other local gospel churches?) and was this different from your demographic as a child?

2.5 What made you consider and then pinpoint planting in this area?

2.4 Describe the process of planting ... Which option most closely fits your experience ...
- pioneering planting from scratch (just you and your family)
- a few committed people from a mother church
- a small to medium group from a mother church
- come into another core group who was already planting.
- another example (please outline).

2.5 How many people did you start with?
- as your initial core group
- at your first public worship meeting

2.6   What was the make-up of the core group (social / cultural / ethnicity, married, single. kids)? Did this reflect the demographic of the area you were planting a church in?

2.7   How far away did the core group live from the meeting place?

2.8   How did you go about selecting or recruiting this core group? (open question)

2.9   Did you plant with a formal church planting network?

2.9.1   If (yes) to a formal planting network what did the support you received look like?
        • financial support
        • training
        • boot camp
        • assessment
        • coaching
        • conferences
        • other (please outline)

2.9.2   If (no) to formal planting network did you receive any other coaching or training?

2.10.1 Open question – describe an average week for you as a church planter ... (approximately how many hours a week would you work? How much time would be spent in making contacts with the community and seeking to witness? How much time within the study? etc)

2.10.2 Open question – describe your role within the church plant ... (for example full time pastor, part time, teacher/visionary, ministry machine (!) etc.)

2.10.3 Is your plant currently still meeting? - yes - no

2.10.4 If no, how long did the plant function before it was closed down?

2.10.5 Who made that decision and why?

2.10.6 Do you think it was too soon or too late?

SECTION 3

3.0   Why do you think the plant did not work as expected? Recognising that situations are always complicated and multifaceted, we would love to know your reflections on why you feel the plant did not work as expected. Please be as honest and give as much information as possible

3.1   Aspects that related to you as a planter?

3.1.1   Character questions (please describe)

3.1.2   Gifting questions (please describe)

3.1.3   Vision questions (please describe)

3.1.4   Spouse and Marriage questions (please describe)

3.1.5   Relational questions – both within the church but also the local community (please describe)

3.1.6   Other ... e.g. issues of leadership, contextualisation, temperament, (please describe)

3.1.7   Which of these would you say was the most important?

3.2   Internal factors within the church...?

3.2.1   Disunity (please describe)

3.2.2   Size of church (please describe)

3.2.3   Lack of programs

3.2.4   Other ... (please describe)

3.2.5   Which of these would you say was the most important?

3.3   External factors from outside the church ...? (Sometimes in God's peculiar providence things 'outside our control' just happen which makes planting impossible)
For example persecution, issues with funding or a tragedy (please describe)

3.4   If you were to pick one main reason as to why the plant did not go as expected what would it be?

3.5   Would others agree with this assessment? If not, what might they say?

SECTION 4

4.0   Reflections

4.1   Did other leaders have a different view as to why the church wasn't viable? If so, what would they say?

4.2   If you were to plant again - how would you do it differently?

4.3   What do you think you've learnt from the experience?
- about yourself (open question)
- about church ministry (open question)
- about church planting (open question).

SECTION 5

5.0   How are you doing now?

5.1   What support have you received in light of this? (please describe)

5.2   Do you feel you have received sufficient support? If not, what would have helped? (please describe)

5.3   Are you in any kind of formal paid ministry context now? (please describe)

5.4   What would be the main lessons you would want to pass on to other church planters?

SECTION 6

6.0   As we seek to analyse findings and help churches plant again in the future, would you be prepared:

6.1   To possibly follow up this survey with a more in depth conversation? - if so please provide an email

6.2   To be quoted in any salient findings with initials and your plant location?

Thanks so much for your help with this.
If you would like to receive a copy of the findings, please let us know.
Every blessing.

APPENDIX 2

Church Unity Questions to Explore

Lots of the disunity came from assumptions and topics that hadn't been discussed until it was too late. These ranged from issues of theology (whether core or secondary (or tertiary)) to practical ministry questions or issues of personality.

Often some of the disunity came from people simply not knowing each other – what things can you do to encourage deep friendships within the new church? Perhaps encourage people to ask questions of each other as you host different social events in the early days.

- Can you tell me how and when you became a Christian?

- What's been your experience of previous churches? What have you appreciated? What's been hard?

- Who's been the single most influential person in your life? Why have you picked them?

- What's been the experience in life that's shaped you the most? Why have you picked this?

- Why have you come to this church plant?

Obviously there are many, many issues that people may disagree over, here are a few questions to begin with.

- How would you share the gospel with someone who's not a believer? What aspects are vital and what are secondary? Why?

- What do you think a church is? What aspects are vital? Why?

- What do you think should be included in a church service? Is there anything that should not be included? How long do you think a service ought to be?

- Do you believe in the ongoing presence of charismatic gifts for today? Why? What role ought they have in church life? Why?

- What role do you think men and women ought to have in church life? Why?

- What mode of baptism do you think is biblical? Why?

- What do you understand by the term 'the sovereignty of God'?

- Can you articulate the vision for this church plant? Do you agree with that vision? What questions do you have?

☙ APPENDIX 3 ☙

Putting together an MOU between the Parent Church and the Church Plant

An MOU is a memorandum of understanding – a (non-binding legal) document that clearly records the details of an agreement between two (or more) parties.

When establishing the ongoing relational parameters between a parent church and church plant, it's important to have clarity over expectations for the ongoing relationship. Note that the Senior Pastor of the parent church may end up moving on and so it's unwise to rely on pre-existing relational capital.

- What exactly will the support entail? (Be specific – pastoral supervision, training, finance, admin help etc)

- Who will receive the support? (the planter? Other leaders?)

- How often will they receive the support? (Weekly? Monthly? Annually?)

- How long will the support last? (1 year, 3 years, 5 years etc)

For example
It has been agreed that

- Senior Pastor Pete, will meet monthly for lunch with Planter Paul for an initial three years. During those monthly meetings, as well as supporting and praying for him, Senior Pastor Pete will give feedback on one of Paul's sermons from that month, as well as discussing together the next chapter from the ministry book that the two have been reading. Pete will also help with any ministry or pastoral questions that Paul is struggling with.

- Every two months the parent church will commit to collecting prayer points and pray on a Sunday morning for the plant, as well as feeding back some of the joys and challenges so far to the main congregation.

- For the first three years the plant will be able to share administrative support - up to three hours per week - in the parent church office. This will include use of the printer and office supplies.

- For the first five years the parent church agrees to help fund the church plant a total of €40,000: €12,000 in year 1, €10,000 in year 2, €8,000 in year 3, €6,000 in year 4 and €4000 in year 5. If the plant is struggling financially there will be a conversation at the end of year 3, over the possibility of more support.

Signatures: ....

....

Other books by Christian Focus Publications:

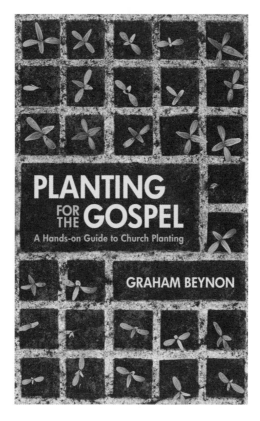

PLANTING
FOR
THE GOSPEL

A Hands-on Guide to Church Planting

GRAHAM BEYNON

Planting for the Gospel

A hands–on Guide to Church Planting

Graham Beynon

To some planting a church seems an impossible dream; others have entirely unrealistic ideals of how easily it can be done. This helpful guide recognises that no church starts out the same and there are several different models that can be followed. Coming from an author with real experience and including real–world case studies from a wide range of settings, this is a tremendously practical and helpful introduction that will lay the foundations for a group of Christian people, a church, to be committed to one another; praying, learning and growing together; seeking to be healthy, flourishing and biblically grounded.

This little book will introduce you to the many different ways that people go about planting churches. Given that the Church is God's chosen instrument to save the world, what could be more important than learning about how new churches can begin?

Adrian Warnock
Author of Raised with Christ and Hope Reborn
and prolific blogger at adrianwarnock.com

ISBN: 978-1-84550-636-0

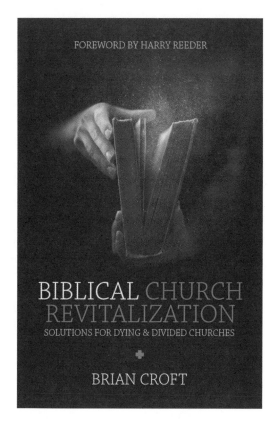

FOREWORD BY HARRY REEDER

BIBLICAL CHURCH
REVITALIZATION
SOLUTIONS FOR DYING & DIVIDED CHURCHES

✦

BRIAN CROFT

Biblical Church Revitalization

Solutions for Dying & Divided Churches

Brian Croft

- Strategy to revitalize dying churches
- Looks at biblical pattern of church planting and strengthening.
- "Definitive resource for rescuing dying churches in our generation."

There is a unique and special power and testimony in not just a vibrant local church full of life, but an old historic one that had lost its way, was on life support, and into which God saw fit to breathe life once again. *Biblical Church Revitalization* calls us to an intentional commitment to church revitalization in the face of dying and divided churches.

I loved this book. Immensely practical and completely realistic. This should be a must read for all pastors and church planters when it comes to handling expectations of the ministry. Very, very good. Get on it.

Mez McConnell
Pastor, Niddrie Community Church
and Ministry Director of 20Schemes

ISBN: 978-1-78191-766-4

Christian Focus Publications

Our mission statement –

STAYING FAITHFUL

In dependence upon God we seek to impact the world through literature faithful to His infallible Word, the Bible. Our aim is to ensure that the Lord Jesus Christ is presented as the only hope to obtain forgiveness of sin, live a useful life and look forward to heaven with Him.

Our books are published in four imprints:

Popular works including biographies, commentaries, basic doctrine and Christian living.

Books representing some of the best material from the rich heritage of the church.

MENTOR

Books written at a level suitable for Bible College and seminary students, pastors, and other serious readers. The imprint includes commentaries, doctrinal studies, examination of current issues and church history.

CF4•K

Children's books for quality Bible teaching and for all age groups: Sunday school curriculum, puzzle and activity books; personal and family devotional titles, biographies and inspirational stories – because you are never too young to know Jesus!

Christian Focus Publications Ltd,
Geanies House, Fearn, Ross-shire,
IV20 1TW, Scotland, United Kingdom.
www.christianfocus.com